Contents

Introduction

Maritime piracy has become a front-burner issue, at least for the media. However, from a strategic military standpoint there are a myriad of multifarious problems, many of which have yet to be resolved. Whatever decisions are derived regarding complex legal and administrative issues, Special Operations Forces (SOF) certainly will play a role with interventions in critical incidents. They also will have interest in the determination of larger international issues regarding counter-piracy and participate in determining effective solutions to crimes committed on the seas. As will be discussed, proposed counter-piracy operations aimed at support structures may require SOF air and land-based elements as well.

This study will examine the problems of piracy on a global basis, but focus on the Horn of Africa (HOA) in particular. Despite extensive international efforts to curtail piracy in the Gulf of Aden, the trend demonstrated continually rising activity through mid-2012. There were a record number of ships taken in 2010, and in 2011 the cost of piracy was estimated at $7 billion.[1] According to a London School of Economics paper by Patrick Cullen, piracy is an exemplary cost-benefit model of business.[2] In the past decade, average ransoms have escalated from around $150,000 per ship and crew in 2005 to well over $5 million per incident.[3] The trend of higher ransom demands continues to grow. In early 2012, it was reported that $170 million was paid out the prior year, and the demands for returning tankers rose to $10 million per vessel.[4] Given the expanse of the Gulf of Aden, over 1.1 million square miles, the probabilities of being captured are relatively small. However, as indicated, the rewards for pirates are potentially very high.

Worth noting is that the International Maritime Bureau reported pirate attacks in the HOA region declined significantly during the latter part of 2012.[5] That decrease was largely because of that a combination of expensive military and industry interventions in the area. However, pirate attacks in other areas of the world have increased.[6] By June of 2013, piracy on the west coast of Africa, especially in the Gulf of Guinea, had risen to the point that it had exceeded the attacks off the HOA.[7] A lucrative crime of opportunity, piracy will flourish whenever and wherever the conditions allow. When suppressed in one area, it will emerge in another.

There are many issues in addition to the cost-benefit ratio of piracy that deserves serious consideration. These include:

- The history of piracy and counter-piracy
- The evolution of piracy from groups of marginally equipped, but dangerous independent thugs, to larger business enterprises attracting criminally complicit investors
- The nexus of piracy and sea borne terrorism
- The emerging role of organized crime in piracy
- The appropriate role for the U.S. military (given that less than two percent of the ships in the region carry American flags)
- The considerations for counter-piracy land operations and other non-sea-based interventions
- The legal issues associated with counter-piracy missions:
  - Jurisdiction and sovereignty on the high seas
  - Evidence collection and presentation
  - Disposition of pirates who are captured
  - Responsibilities for costs associated with trial and incarceration
  - Use of capital punishment
- The true costs of piracy
- Appropriate roles for SOF intervention
- The measures that can be taken to counter the effects of piracy (beyond military intervention)

It is known that pirates, especially in the HOA region, have been evolving their tactics and responding to the international counter-piracy efforts put forth by combined naval forces. This monograph will speculate on the logical extrapolation of their capabilities in light of cooperative efforts between mercenary pirates and ideological structures such as al-Qaeda and Associated Movements (AQAM) and a global jihad as postulated by Richard Shultz in *Strategic Culture and Strategic Studies: An Alternative Framework for Assessing al-Qaeda and the Global Jihad Movement*.[8] The excogitative implications of such escalation would be quite significant for military planners and policymakers.

Definition

For current legal purposes, according to the United Nations (UN) Convention on the Law of the Seas, piracy is defined as consisting of any of the following acts:

    (a) Any illegal acts of violence or detention, or any act of depredation, committed for private ends by the crew or the passengers of a private ship or a private aircraft, and directed:

        (i) on the high seas, against another ship or aircraft, or against persons or property on board such ship or aircraft;

        (ii) against a ship, aircraft, persons or property in a place outside the jurisdiction of any State;

    (b) any act of voluntary participation in the operation of a ship or of an aircraft with knowledge of facts making it a pirate ship or aircraft;

    (c) any act of inciting or of intentionally facilitating an act described in subparagraph (a) or (b).[9]

It is noted that there are several definitions of piracy, and some researchers now argue that there is a need to expand the language to include acts of terrorism on the high seas.[10]

> *It is noted that there are several definitions of piracy, and some researchers now argue that there is a need to expand the language to include acts of terrorism on the high seas.*

The UN definition also includes the hijacking of aircraft as an act of piracy. The convention does account for warships in which the crew has mutinied and a range of other circumstances including responsibilities for handling of ships that are boarded and found not to have been pirated.[11] That will be addressed later when considering the legal consequences of counter-piracy operations.

Centuries ago, some pirates were contracted by governments to support their war activities. Lacking official navies, it was an expedient method of adding a seaborne dimension to their military capabilities. Under that process, those *pirates* became *privateers*, affording them a different legal status. That practice was outlawed in the treaty of Peace of Westphalia in 1648.

There are inherent inequities when comparing various types of piracy. While this monograph addresses maritime piracy, it is important to remember that the word is also commonly used in several other venues. The theft of intellectual property ranks high as a serious problem and extends to all facets of visual, auditory, and printed media. The term has also been applied to counterfeit goods of various kinds. The most problematic is the manufacturing of fake prescription pharmaceutical products. Like piracy on the high seas, piracy of prescription pharmaceuticals has lethal consequences. Each year those counterfeit drugs kill thousands of people; orders of magnitude more than are killed in pirate attacks against shipping.[12] That piracy, however, fails to draw the same level of media attention. That is a point to consider when strategic importance and commitment of resources are discussed. Even maritime piracy can extend into unanticipated venues. For example, there are people who deem illegal fishing in restricted waters as piracy.[13]

1. History of Maritime Piracy

Piracy has been a human endeavor as long as people have been seafaring. The concentration of international counter-piracy efforts in the Gulf of Aden off the Somali coast is relatively new. Well over three millennia ago, around 1400 BCE, pirates roamed the Mediterranean. The first reports are of Lukka sea raiders attacking ships in Asia Minor and later becoming allies of the Hittites. For the next millennia, as the major civilizations grew in the Mediterranean, all encountered or used pirates in the local conflicts. The Phoenician and Greek Sailors complained of pirates as did the Minoans. However, some groups also used pirates to their advantage in waging war. Counter-piracy operations were undertaken by the Athenians, Carthaginians, and Romans.[14]

While tales of piracy on the Mediterranean constitute the early reports, it has been a global blight leaving few waters unscathed. The best known cases in American mythology are the highly romanticized exploits of the pirates of the Caribbean. Somewhat perversely, Hollywood productions have managed to transmogrify the public image of pirates from the ruthless, murdering scavengers, and amoral thugs that they were, into affable, albeit somewhat misguided, scoundrels.

For many years, pirates did roam the Caribbean, sometimes with authorization from foreign governments and operating as privateers. They began marauding in the 16th century and continued until around 1720. For the most part they were able to function because of the lawlessness in the region, a factor they have in common with today's pirates. This led to what has become known as *The Golden Age of Piracy*, which is surely a misnomer.[15]

The European exploration and exploitation of the New World facilitated piracy. In settling the Americas, the leaders of all countries wanted goods shipped back to their home ports. The tales of Spanish galleons laden with gold and other treasures were well known. Traveling alone soon proved too dangerous as the wealth they carried was a tempting target. However, even sailing in convoys did not guarantee security from heavily armed and fast moving pirates. During that time, the near constant wars in Europe spilled over into the region. The slave trade also became important, as the indigenous population of the exploited areas did not fare well when they came in contact with disease carried by the European explorers and settlers. By some estimates, over 90 percent of the native population died from these epidemic diseases. Thus, needing hands to work mines and fields, slaves from Africa were imported in substantial numbers. The slave ships were also tempting targets for pirates.[16]

Another well-known historical hotspot for piracy was the Barbary Coast reigning terror from bases in the southern Mediterranean. Rising during the 16th century, the Barbary pirates attacked targets both on the high seas and the lightly defended coastal areas. Conducted as a business, the pirates were financed by capitalists and paid tribute to the local leaders who allowed them to plunder at will. In addition to stealing treasure, the Barbary pirates also kidnapped many victims. Those who had access to wealth were allowed to pay ransom. The less fortunate captives were sold into slavery. There was an estimate that at one time more than 20,000 prisoners were being held in Algeria alone.[17] During the entire reign of terror, it is estimated that more than a million Europeans were captured and taken as slaves to North Africa.[18]

While many of the Barbary pirate galleys were confined to the Mediterranean Sea, some crews obtained vessels capable of roaming the Atlantic. There are reports of them raiding ports in Ireland and as far away as Iceland. For many decades they practiced their trade which was so pervasive that it had significant impact on international commerce. Some countries simply paid extortion in return for safe passage. From the pragmatic standpoint, appeasement was considered less expensive than funding the effort to fight the pirates. Unfortunately, the pirates sometimes disregarded their agreements and captured ships anyway.

The Barbary pirates did not operate in a strategic vacuum. With periodic wars throughout Europe and the power of the Ottoman Empire, the actions of pirates were sometimes viewed as politically useful to one side or another. Tiring of paying ransom and being raided, most of the major powers sent naval forces against these pirates. These were not a concerted effort to stamp out piracy, but rather designed to serve their country's interests at that moment.

The fledgling United States was brought into the fray in the Mediterranean for both geopolitical and economic reasons. Having been squeezed out of the Caribbean, and having poor relations with Great Britain, new trade was necessary. Prior to American independence, the treaties signed by the British had covered the ships sailing from North America as part of their fleet. Following in the tradition of European nations, America did begin paying tribute to the Barbary Coastal states in order to secure and maintain open sea lanes. Over time the monetary demands increased, and ships were seized with additional ransom extorted.[19]

As Secretary of State, Thomas Jefferson counseled against paying tribute. Left unprotected, U.S. vessels became targets. In 1794, pirates took 11 ships and captured 115 crew members. That led to the Naval Act of 1794 which authorized the building of a navy.[20] Conflicts continued for the next several years. Treaties were made and broken. Later, as President, Jefferson initiated four years of war with the state sponsors of the pirates. The then-recently established U.S. Navy, while not winning every battle, did prove to be a formidable adversary. Actions by Commodore Edward Preble convinced Morocco to leave the fight, and his shelling of Tripoli proved effective, at least temporarily. Then American land forces threatened to take Tripoli and install a new leader. Finally, in 1815 naval victories by Commodore William Bainbridge and Commodore Stephen Decatur led to treaties that effectively ended the power of the Barbary pirates.[21]

Operating away from most Americans' attention are the pirates of the South China Sea. However, given the recent realignment of national defense priorities and greater attention being given to the Asia-Pacific region, piracy there is likely to attract more attention in the future. In fact, the South China Sea, encompassing over 3.5 million square kilometers, has experienced a piracy problem for hundreds of years. It is reported that for nearly half of the period from 1520 to 1810, "pirates dominated the seas" in that area of the world. Pervasive and problematic, the Chinese currently describe pirates as "the enemy of the human race."[22]

2. Contemporary Piracy

Piracy in that area has never stopped, though it has been eclipsed by the rampant activities originating near Somalia. Rather than the high profit attacks that make current news, from the late 1970s and 1980s there were many tales of local pirates terrorizing boat people who fled for their lives from Vietnam and Cambodia. Stealing their victim's meager possessions, rape and murder at the hands of Thai pirates was the fate that befell thousands of these unfortunate people.[23]

Incidents of piracy continued to climb in the 1990s, and a majority of them were reported in or near the South China Sea, especially near the Strait of Malacca. The International Maritime Bureau complained that many of the pirates were operating with impunity from small ports along the southern China coast.[24] That assertion is denied by China, and the consequences for being convicted of "robbery at sea," as the Chinese refer to piracy, can be extremely severe, as will be discussed later in this paper.

Most papers on this topic note the problems associated with the Strait of Malacca where piracy has been practiced for hundreds of years. The number of attacks since the end of World War II is not known, and many, if not most, have gone unreported. Some ships were boarded while they were docked at local ports, but the more frequent scenario was that five to ten pirates would attack in the darkness, between approximately 1a.m. to 6 a.m. Using grappling hooks, they would climb up and take over the ship. The intent was to snatch any money and material that could be easily transported and depart as quickly as possible. The entire operation might last a few hours, but could be completed in as little as 30 minutes. The usual take was $10,000-20,000, extremely small by today's standards.[25]

As a result of the increased activity and the impact it was having on the Asian financial markets, a comprehensive program was designed and considerable pressure brought to bear on the pirates. This was the *Regional Cooperation Agreement on Combating Piracy and Armed Robbery against Ships in Asia*. The effects of this will be covered later, but the efforts did reduce the incidents of piracy dramatically.[26]

As Indonesia cracked down on piracy, the attacks in the HOA became far more active and attracted global attention. Though under reported, piracy off the coast of Somalia has increased at an alarming rate. Most incidents are noticed only by the International Maritime Bureau. However, a few dramatic attacks have caused concern. One such incident was about 50 pirates taking the Ukrainian cargo ship *Faina* on 25 September 2008. What made that raid so special was the *Faina's* cargo—and included 33 T-72 Russian tanks plus other war-making material.[27] The ship was headed to Mombasa, but it was believed that cargo was to be transshipped to Juba, the capital of what became South Sudan in 2011. Because of the weapons involved, naval ships from several countries gave chase but were not successful in catching it. Negotiation lasted for months. After a reported $3.2 million ransom was paid, on 6 February 2009 the ship and its crew of 20 were set free. Unfortunately, the captain had suffered a fatal stroke while in captivity. Worth noting is that the original ransom demand was for $20 million dollars.[28]

Another game-changing hijacking about the same time was the capture of the Sirius Star on 17 November 2008. The vessel was a huge crude-oil supertanker with capacity to carry 2.2 million barrels of oil. Sailing southeast of Kenya, it was 520 miles at sea and not in waters believed to be at risk.[29] At that time, this was the farthest that the pirates had ventured from Somalia. The captured supertanker was taken to the port of Eyl in northeast Somalia and ransom demanded. The value of the cargo was estimated at over $100 million, and the ship was worth another $150 million. The first ransom demanded for the Saudi-owned ship was for $25 million. About a week later, the demand dropped to $15 million, and on 9 January 2009, they released the Sirius Star and the 25 crewmembers reportedly for $3 million. This was dropped by parachute onto the deck, thus eliminating any need for a face-to-face meeting between the pirates and representatives paying for the release.

By the end of the ordeal, it appears that there were at least 20 pirates involved. Several of them in this case were not as lucky as others. After leaving the Sirius Star in a small boat, they capsized in a storm. Five of the eight pirates on board drowned, taking their money with them. One body did wash ashore with a plastic bag containing $153,000.[30] This information provides insight into how ransom is divided immediately among the pirates. It appears they do not trust each other, and the distribution of substantial amounts of money is accomplished in a rather unrefined manner. This may be an important point when considering countermeasures attempting to interrupt their financial system.

Not all of the targets have been large cargo ships. The taking of the 288 foot French sailing ship, Le Pocant, in February 2009, was strictly orchestrated for hostage taking. This luxury craft was transiting the area en route to the Mediterranean and capable of only 13 knots when it was besieged by young pirates in faster skiffs. The captain did get out a distress call, and the heavily-armed Canadian frigate, H.M.C.S. Charlottetown, was quickly on the scene shadowing them. Still, the pirates, armed only with Kalashnikovs, were able to hold rescuers at bay by threats to kill the hostages.[31] They were followed for a week, and eventually the hostages were all released after a reported $2.15 million ransom was paid. As it happened, only crew members had been on board at the time of the incident. The Le Pocant's normal passengers are people of substantial wealth. Capture of such passengers would likely have changed the demands considerably. Once the transfer of hostages was made, the French military went into action. The reports of casualties are conflicting, but several pirates were captured, and helicopters fired on the others as they retreated on land.[32]

No area of the world is immune from piracy, and not all happens on the high seas. The mighty Amazon River has hosted pirates for a long time, and the use of violence is a norm. In 2011, the problems caused on the waterway rose to a level that caused the Brazilian government to create a new counter-piracy force.[33] The targets are usually passenger boats with the intent to rob the people as opposed to ransom or taking cargo. The large boats can carry up to 300 passengers, all of whom may become targeted. It is not uncommon for the pirates to threaten to shoot passengers if their demands are not met. Creating the feeling of terror is part of their agenda.

> *No area of the world is immune from piracy, and not all happens on the high seas.*

The Amazon image is still tarred by the 2001 killing of New Zealand's Sir Peter Blake, one of the world's most famous sailors and renowned environmentalist. Blake was shot by a group of armed pirates known as "the water rats" in a night-time robbery on his boat anchored at Macapá, Brazil, in the delta at the mouth of the Amazon. Because of Blake's stature, the incident resulted in global headlines. On the Pacific side of South America, Peru has experienced a small but increasing number of pirate attacks. In, March 2011, for example, a Japanese fishing trawler was boarded late at night though the approach was very low-tech. The crew stated the pirates arrived via rowboats. Here again the target was personal property and money.[34]

While the massive number of incidents of piracy in the HOA is well know, other areas of the continent have serious problems as well. There have been numerous attacks originating on the west coast, especially in Nigeria. In fact, some reports estimate that the problem, which is rapidly increasing, is nearly as serious as the incidents off Somalia. They also indicate that the actual number is underreported as the targets are often transporting illegal material.[35] In early 2012, the International Maritime Bureau noticed the increase in activity in West Africa and indicated that Nigeria and Benin were becoming "piracy hotspots."[36] In Gulf of Guinea, chemical-laden cargo vessels are favorite targets for criminal attacks. Of specific concern is that these attacks have a higher rate of violence than others in the region. One difference between piracy on the east and west coasts of Africa is intent. In the HOA, pirates focus on capturing the crews and ships, holding them for ransom. On the west coast, pirates attack ships with the main intent of stealing the cargo. They offload the cargo onto waiting vessels and move the goods to shore to be sold on the black market. This is a much easier operation as there is no need for negotiations or the detaining and maintenance of the crews for long periods of time.

As reported in *Africa: Irregular Warfare on the Dark Continent*, Nigeria has significant instability problems. Many of those issues have amplified since that document was published in 2009.[37] In the north, the Islamic militant group Boko Haram has been engaged in numerous bombings, mostly aimed at Christians in the area.[38,39] The intensity of the conflict was such that security companies rated the level of threat in Nigeria as on par with Afghanistan. The problems at sea have also intensified. In 2012, a substantial increase in piracy attacks was noted against shipping goods and crude oil containers in the Gulf of Guinea. Previously, the Movement for the Emancipation of the Nigerian Delta pirates made raids by small boats conducting low-level robberies of fishing and passenger boats. Now these pirates are attacking ocean-going vessels well out on international waters.[40]

As noted in the title, the piracy business can be very lucrative. This is not a new phenomenon, and some pirates have become incredibly wealthy. In 2008, Forbes published a list of top performing pirates. They amortized booty based on historical records from the period against the dollar value in that year. The rock star was Black Sam Bellamy, who plundered the New England coast in the 18th century accumulating an estimated $120 million. The capture of the slave ship Whydah in 1717 reportedly yielded him four and a half tons of gold and silver. British privateer Sir Francis Drake, operating at the behest of the Queen of England, was in second place and brought in about $115 million, while Thomas Tew ranked third with $102 million in his collection. The infamous Edward "Blackbeard" Teach was down the list at tenth place and only stole $12.5 million but there are indications he had other loot that was unaccounted for in the records.[41]

It is natural that the majority of U.S. military publications concerning maritime piracy are found in U.S. Navy journals and many contain small sections on history. For those readers interested in learning far more about the history of piracy, highly recommended for future research is the Naval War College Newport Paper 35, Piracy and Maritime Crime: Historical and Modern Case Studies for a wealth of information on the topic.[42]

3. SOF Hostage Rescue Missions

In recent years, there have been two high-profile SOF counter-piracy interventions that have catapulted attention into the public domain. The first involved the rescue of Captain Richard Phillips following a five-day standoff in the Indian Ocean. On 8 April 2009, pirates attacked and boarded the American cargo ship Maersk Alabama—with 17,000 metric tons of cargo bound for Mombasa, Kenya—while it was 240 nautical miles at sea. Given some warning, the Chief Engineer Mike Perry, and 14 members of the crew were able to get into a secure room. With assistance, Perry was able to swamp the pirate's boat and take control of the engine, steering away from the bridge. They then successfully shut down all of the ship's systems, thus preventing the pirates from having the vessel sailed to Somalia.[43]

Chief Engineer Perry left the security of the barricaded room in an attempt to rescue the sailors who had not made it to safety. The U.S. Navy quickly interceded, and the USS Bainbridge arrived on the scene staying just a few hundred meters from the Maersk Alabama. Unable to control the ship, and having lost their skiff, the pirates took Phillips and departed on a lifeboat. Other pirates off the coast of Somalia holding many more captives heard of the plight of their kin and began to head to the area where their relatives were in trouble. However, the significant U.S. naval presence in the region, which included the USS Halyburton, USS Boxer, and USS Bainbridge, convinced them to stay away.

Figure 1. A team from the amphibious assault ship USS Boxer tows the lifeboat from the Maersk Alabama to the Boxer to be processed for evidence after the successful rescue of Merchant Marine Capt. Richard Phillips. U.S. Navy photo by Petty Officer 2nd Class Jon Rasmussen.

The days of delay and communications with special Federal Bureau of Investigation (FBI) hostage negotiators provided time for SOF elements to be brought to the scene from the United States. U.S. Navy SEALs joined the USS Bainbridge where they could observe the pirates, armed with AK-47s, threatening the lone hostage. On 12 April, one pirate, Abdiwali Abdiqadir Muse, was allowed on board the USS Bainbridge to arrange the terms for ransom of Captain Phillips. While he was there, the SEAL snipers watching events on the lifeboat took an opportunity in which all three of the remaining pirates were visible and exposed. With near simultaneous shots they eliminated all of them.[44] In reviewing the events, it was stated that the threatening actions toward Captain Phillips by one of the pirates necessitated the action. Those who have reviewed this case acknowledge the extraordinary skill required to execute this mission at sea and with dwindling light conditions. Immediately following the shooting, the teenaged Abdiwali Abdiqadir Muse was arrested. He was brought to New York for trial and determined to be an adult. On 16 February 2011, he was sentenced to 33 years and nine months imprisonment.[45]

Somali pirates do not necessarily confine their activities to maritime operations. In January 2012, more headlines proclaimed an epic rescue in Somalia, again conducted by SEALs. The daring operation commenced with a high-altitude parachute jump from altitudes "high enough to avoid puncturing the nighttime silence."[46] Once on the ground, the team moved to an encampment where the two hostages were known to be held. The timing of the mission was predicated on reports of the deteriorating health of Jessica Buchanan, a 32-year-old American aid worker. Also rescued was Poul Hagen Thisted, a 60-year-old Danish coworker in demining operations who had been kidnapped at the same time as Buchanan.[47]

> While there have been other less visible operations conducted by SOF elements, both of these events exemplify the most recent addition to SOF truths: "Most special operations require non-SOF assistance."

While few tactical details were made public, it is known that the team entered the camp near Hiimo Graabo and encountered a number of kidnappers. A firefight ensued, and nine armed men were left dead. Local sources report that five bandits were captured but none returned, a claim denied by officials. It was noted that planning did provide for the taking of prisoners should any be captured. The SEAL team and the freed hostages quickly were exfiltrated via Army helicopters and taken to Camp Lemonnier in Djibouti.[48]

While there have been other less visible operations conducted by SOF elements, both of these events exemplify the most recent addition to SOF truths: "Most special operations require non-SOF assistance."[49]

Despite the press emphasis on the SEAL snipers, in the Maersk Alabama rescue, most of the activity was undertaken by conventional naval forces with interagency support from the FBI. As mentioned, the rescue of Buchanan and Thisted was based on health concerns. Intelligence elements had been able to remotely monitor Buchanan's status and provide the team with critical information about what to expect on the ground.

This action also had political significance. Partially due to circumstance, the raid happened immediately before the President's State of the Union Address. Widely reported was President Obama's impromptu remark to then Secretary of Defense Leon Panetta as he entered the chamber of the House of Representatives. In addition, the President formally advised Congress that the raid had been conducted.[50] It is a rarity that specific operations are formally conveyed to Congress by the President.

There are reports that the greedy pirates had refused an offer of $1.5 million for the release of those hostages. Other American hostages have not fared as well. At the time of the rescue event, an American reporter was being held by pirates near the coast.[51] There were reports that the pirates holding him had begun moving him frequently to avoid being targeted. They also threatened to kill him if additional actions were taken.[52]

However successful some counter-piracy operations have been, they also have resulted in adverse unintended consequences. On 22 February 2011, four American hostages held near Somalia were executed as negotiations to gain their release failed. Not a crew from a cargo ship, these sailors were on a private yacht, Quest, circumnavigating the world preaching and passing out Bibles. The USS Sterett, a guided missile destroyer, was a few hundred meters away when a rocket-propelled grenade (RPG) was fired in its direction. Gunfire erupted on the yacht, and SOF elements were deployed. They killed two pirates and captured 13 others. Unfortunately, they were too late to save the hostages.[53] This incident represented the first time that Americans had been killed by pirates in the Gulf of Aden.

4. Recent Evolution of Piracy

Over time, the tactics, techniques, and technology available to the pirates off Somalia have changed. Initially, groups of local thugs armed with the abundant weapons that have proliferated from the decades of irregular warfare in the area would obtain a small boat and attack targets of opportunity. Using grappling hooks and ropes and armed with AK-47s and RPGs, it was not difficult for them to board slow-moving and unprotected commercial ships. The word quickly spread that the targets were relatively easy to capture, and that shipping companies were willing to pay ransom to obtain the freedom of their ships and crew.

Addressing the U.S. House of Representatives Committee on Foreign Affairs, Rear Admiral William Baumgartner of the U.S. Coast Guard noted that even after being captured, pirates often escape prosecution and return to their illegal activities. The payment of ransom, Rear Admiral Baumgartner stated, entices more pirates to engage in a "criminal, but highly successful, business model; pirating vessels and demanding huge ransoms."[54]

International pressure has had some modest effect in countering pirate attacks in the HOA region. After four consecutive years in which attacks rose, in 2011 there were 439 reported attacks compared to 445 in 2010. The he number of crew members taken hostage dropped from 1,181 in 2010 to 802 in 2011. Deaths of hostages remained at eight for both years.[55] The vast majority of the attacks in the world occurred off either East or West Africa. Most attempts were not successful on actually boarding the targeted ship. The decline is believed to be at least partially due to preemptive strikes against "Pirate Action Groups," as well as hardening efforts by the commercial shipping industry.

There are other indications that pirates are becoming more organized and sophisticated. Following personal investigation, Senator Mark Kirk found that Somali-based pirates are organized based on clan structure with no single strategy or chain of command. By operating independently and with a decentralized structure, pirate organizations are extremely difficult to infiltrate and dismantle. It was reported that there are approximately 10 of these organizations with complex financing and operational frameworks. Amazingly, they indicated that private stock markets are functioning where pirate groups seek investors to bankroll their operations in exchange for a cut of the ransom. Additionally, he indicated that pirate networks are starting to adopt a military organizational structure to improve their efficiency.[56] This supports the earlier notion that there are people now who invest in piracy by financing mother ships and more expensive equipment. They have also established a system in which one group boards the target, then brings it to a specified port to be held. There they are joined by additional criminals to assist in guard duties and other tasks such as feeding hostages. It even has been indicated that people are assigned to deliver a constant supply of khat, an amphetamine-like stimulant, which is said to cause excitement and commonly used in Somalia.

The level of influence pirates have is exemplified by the placement of Garaad Mohamed, a Somali kingpin, as number four on the Lloyds of London list of people controlling the shipping industry. He boasts of controlling more than 200 pirate crews and indicates more are joining him all the time. He has been associated with many hijackings including the Ukrainian ship Faina, which contained the Russian tanks, and the Sirius Star oil tanker.[57]

Noteworthy was the capture of a group of 10 criminals en route to the Italian-flagged *MT Enrico Levoli* which was hijacked on 27 December 2011 near the coast of Oman and brought back to Somalia. Among those arrested were investors who had been going to check on their prize which included 18 hostages.[58] An important aspect of this counter-piracy operation was that it was conducted successfully by Somali police. That is indicative that programs designed to increase capacity of the countries experiencing a high volume of piracy can be effective. It should also be noted that the arrests of those 10 did not end that hijacking incident. The *Enrico Levoli* finally was released and sailed for Italy on 24 April 2012.[59] It is unknown if a ransom was paid, but there is a high probability that it was.

One disturbing incident in August 2012 signaled an escalation of violence by pirates. It involved the bargaining for release of the *MV Orna* and crew a United Arab Emirates-owned cargo ship hijacked in December 2010 off the Seychelles. As the pirates grew weary of the drawn-out negotiations, they executed one crew member in order to demonstrate their resolve. They also threatened to kill more hostages if demands were not met promptly. That was the first time a hostage had been killed as part of ransom negotiations.[60] The tactic worked, and the ship was released in October 2012 after the owners delivered $600,000.[61] Even after the ransom money was paid, the pirates continued to hold some of the crewmembers captive. No additional ransom was paid, but it was not until January 2013 the last of them were released.[62]

Just as counter-piracy operations have changed, so have the actions of the pirates. While the pirates boarding ships may be relatively uneducated, the same is not true for those called "kingpins." It is the kingpins that call the shots and facilitate the actual attacks, most often from their bases safely on land. Recent U.S. policy has identified them as a specific target of interest. The Department of State (DOS) noted counter-piracy objectives, "includes key figures of criminal networks involved in piracy who illicitly plan, organize, facilitate, or finance and profit from such attacks."[63]

These kingpins can be quite sophisticated and technology savvy. They have been using the Internet to track cargo ships and naval activities to determine which vessels are carrying armed guards and which are taking a chance without them.[64] There has been concern about public access to this data for several years. While there has been condemnation of that activity, the data are currently available to anyone with Internet capability. All that is required is a computer operator with Internet access to search for a ship's name. These cyber spies and pirate support personnel can instantly obtain the vessel's location and heading as well as the port the ship last left and their current destination. Considerable information about the nature of the target is readily available on those websites.[65]

Under International Maritime Organization rules, ships normally transmit Automatic Identification System signals to avoid accidents at sea.[66] The captains have an option to turn the equipment off if its use is thought to make a ship vulnerable. In heavily trafficked areas, the danger of collision will likely take precedence over concerns about pirates. There is concern that some ships may try to bluff and indicate they have guards when they do not. Stopping transmission is a practice that the industry deems ill-advised. One countermeasure employed by pirates is to test potential targets. This is accomplished by approaching at a safe distance and firing at the intended victim. They anticipate that if there are armed guards on board, they will return fire rather quickly. If the ship does not return fire, the pirates assume it is safe to attempt to board their prize.

At a cost to governments of over a billion dollars, combined naval forces have had a direct impact on piracy initiated in the HOA.[67] However, West African waters have seen a surge in such activities.[68] In fact, pirate attacks more than doubled in that area between 2011 and 2012 and are now second only to those off Somalia. The objectives of the pirates are different in that the focus is on capturing the cargo and reselling it on the black market. The West African pirates also are becoming more organized and sometimes have smaller ships waiting at predetermined locations to receive the goods. Unlike holding the ship for months or years, the victims are held for seven to ten days while trans-loading takes place.[69] Economics plays a significant role in West African piracy as well. Poverty is rampant in the area, and a majority of the 31 million people in the area live on less than $1 per day. A single shipment can bring in a million dollars on the black market, making the criminal activity very attractive.[70] While the U.S. Navy does conduct counter-piracy training for Nigerian naval forces, the efforts pale compared to those in Somalia. The combined naval forces of the entire region are totally inadequate to stem the increased piracy activity. The level of violence by the West African pirates has been noted as a concern to mariners.[71]

The actual number of recent attacks is not known. It is estimated that most ship owners do not report the incidents as that could lead to higher insurance premiums. Oil tankers are prized, and it is alleged that Nigerian officials and oil company insiders sometimes advise pirates of the cargo movements ahead of time. As the economy is based on oil, Nigeria has been hard hit by massive thefts. An estimated $5 billion worth of oil was stolen in that country last year, both on land and through piracy.[72] One thing different about piracy in West Africa is the presence of organized crime in Nigeria, which provides an infrastructure that will be most dangerous, and activity is expected to increase in the near term.[73] As happened in the HOA, when piracy was on the upswing, improved capabilities such as mother-ships and tankers have been added, thus allowing them to attack at more distant locations. Very worrisome is the potential nexus of illegal drugs, organized crime, expanding Islamic extremism, corruption, and oil piracy, all of which are occurring in West Africa.[74]

Oil workers on off-shore rigs have been periodically targeted for kidnapping. While the West African pirates have primarily targeted cargo, it appears they are willing to include kidnap for ransom. In February 2013, pirates took six sailors hostage and demanded over a million dollars for their release. This could portend a shift in focus, or simply additional criminal activity that proves lucrative.[75] In 2012, over 200 hostages were kidnapped in maritime activities in the region.

West Africa is not the only area that has experienced a recent increase in piracy. Such activity in the waters of Southeast Asia have had changes as well. As increased pressure was brought to bear on pirates close to the coast in the Strait of Malacca, it appears they simply moved to deeper water to attack shipping. All of the conditions that support piracy are present in the area and a substantial raise in attacks has been noted.[76]

Far below international scrutiny are the attacks on fishing vessels in many other waters. As an example, the pirates of Khulna, Bangladesh have been creating havoc in the lightly patrolled Bay of Bengal. They are known to steal cargo, including fish and timber, hold boats for ransom, and even poach endangered animals. Neither India nor Bangladesh have applied the resources to interdict these pirates.[77] Like pirates in other areas, extreme poverty and ungoverned spaces allow these practices to continue. In fact, fish piracy is a global problem that is growing as harvesting technology improves and stocks are diminished. The amounts of fish taken illegally are in the millions of tons and have economic impact on countries that heavily rely on that industry.[78] While such piracy currently is not a SOF concern, the magnitude of the problem is worth noting as it can contribute to international tensions, not only in southern Asia, but around the world. This form of piracy may be an issue for the maritime counterparts that SOF operators advise in foreign nations.

5. Legal Aspects

There are numerous complicated legal issues associated with prosecuting pirates. From a U.S. perspective, Navy Judge Advocate General Captain David Iglesias noted that our laws regarding piracy are 150 years old.[79] He stated that much of the problem is lack of consequences when pirates are caught. This is often due to flag state legislative gaps and lack of judicial capacity. Where the acts occur makes a difference in criminal definition as well as jurisdiction. If pirates are operating in littoral waters that are claimed by a nation, the crime and legal disposition are the responsibility of that country. Of course, one reason that piracy has been prevalent in certain areas of the world has been because of weak governance—or, as in the Barbary situation, complicity by local governments.

As Captain Iglesias indicated, the legal system for dealing with piracy is a morass. Capturing pirates is the easy part. The questions that then emerge include: Who will investigate the case? Who will prosecute and in what venue? Where will the suspects be held, and who is responsible for them during incarceration? What evidence is required for conviction? Do the victims have to be present to testify against the pirates?[80]

American law on piracy is covered under *Title 18, Chapter 81 of the U.S. Code.* It prescribes life imprisonment for foreign pirates who are captured in the act. However, that provision only applies if the piracy is against a ship flagged in the U.S. It does not apply for pirates attacking vessels flagged in other nations.[81] Considering that less than one percent of the ships sailing in the Gulf of Aden are U.S.-flagged, it means that very few of the incidents of piracy come under American jurisdiction for prosecution. The flag of the ship is important as an armed encounter on the high seas is bound by the laws of the flagging country. That is unless the encounter occurs in territorial waters, in which case the laws of the territorial state may apply and vary from country to country.[82] Both criminal and civil jurisdiction are very complex and have yet to be totally resolved.

The *United Nations Law of the Seas Convention* covers piracy but enjoins naval vessels from firing on pirates without boarding the ship and confirming that to be the case. These actions are risky but required. They are usually performed by traditional naval forces. The same restrictions apply for ships suspected transporting slaves.[83] Notably, the U.S. is not a signatory to this treaty though most others countries are.[84] As of this writing, 162 countries and the European Union (EU) have ratified the treaty since 1994. Supported by both President Obama and his predecessor President Bush, the Senate continues to block the treaty. Former Secretary of Defense Panetta and Chairman of the Joint Chiefs of Staff General Martin Dempsey emphasized the security benefits, arguing that the treaty provides a mechanism for resolving disputes over strategically important waterways like the Strait of Hormuz. Past and present Department of Defense leaders state that the treaty would strengthen U.S. naval power. It would provide Americans favorable navigational rights and, if necessary, the ability to use military force.[85] Among the advantages gained are the right of transit through international straits and the right of passage through foreign territorial seas.

Also at stake are negotiations for petroleum and mining rights in international waters, and competition for access to the resources of the Arctic Ocean are heating up.[86] Germaine to piracy, the treaty does give each country control of their seas for 200 nautical miles as an exclusive economic zone.[87] That also establishes their right to prosecute pirates operating in those waters. When their acts take place in international waters other laws apply, but they are unevenly enforced. Captured pirates are to be taken to the nearest port and turned over to that jurisdiction for trial. For most pirates operating near Somalia, that port would be Mombasa, Kenya, which is a major shipping center for Eastern Africa.

Of course there are costs associated with both incarceration and trial, and they are not insignificant. As a relatively poor country, Kenya is not well equipped financially to incorporate and absorb those costs. In addition, if the pirates are to be placed on trial, then forensic evidence must be collected and maintained. Much of that evidence comes from the vessel and crew that are the victims of the attack. While meeting the legal requirements for presentation in court, much of what needs to be done is both impractical and counter to the business interests of the ship owners.

Cargo vessels that have been pirated have already been inconvenienced and lost money due to delays in transshipment of goods. Further delays add more cost to their business. Sailors are a transient lot and make money by being at sea. Trials are not held quickly, thus if their testimony is needed in court, they must be returned at the time of the court proceedings. Far worse is that most captured pirates are set free without trial. The Congressional Research Service reported, "Some suggest that a perception of impunity exists among pirates and financiers; nine out of ten Somali pirates apprehended by naval patrols are reportedly released because no jurisdiction is prepared to prosecute them."[88]

Historically, captured pirates were dispatched rather quickly. Those that were given a trial were often hung from the yardarm or another visible location as a reminder to others who might want to ply their trade. There have been reports of capital punishment being meted out in recent years, sometimes on the spot. There are multiple credible reports of pirates being captured and executed at sea, or being released without navigation equipment or other life support.[89] While these actions have been officially denied, it appears very likely to have happened. There are videos available of a pirate ship being scuttled after capture and no record of prisoners being arrested or turned over for prosecution. Aware that summary execution is a politically sensitive issue, releasing a disabled vessel may be considered an acceptable alternative, though the outcome is the same. That, however, would be a violation of the Law of the Sea that requires helping sailors in distress. China has also executed pirates, albeit after a trial for situations in which murder was also included as a charge.[90]

Christina Geisert, Lead Intelligence Analyst U.S. Coast Guard Intelligence Coordination Center, noted, "Sometimes it is hard to distinguish the difference between a maritime crime and an act of piracy, since both are challenging to designate, are based on location and description, and are often incorrectly attributed."[91] While piracy is often considered as a separate category, in reality it is a juxtaposition of a number of crimes. The simple act of boarding a vessel is just the beginning. That will probably involve aggravated assault often followed by kidnapping for ransom which may include torture of victims. Extortion, money laundering, illegal arms trade, and many other offenses may be included in the incident.[92] While piracy has universal jurisdiction and can be prosecuted by any country, these sub-elements vary from country to country.

As Geisert goes on to note, "Analysts charged with the responsibility of tracking reported threats and trends of piracy and maritime crime may become confused with the differences in term characterization."[93] Clearly, if even the analysts whose job it is to track these

While piracy has universal jurisdiction and can be prosecuted by any country, these sub-elements vary from country to country.

incidents have a difficult time distinguishing differences, then the overall reporting may be skewed.

Strangely, some military counter-piracy activities have been used in the defense of the pirates. Lawyers defending some of the pirates captured and charged with murder in the 2011 Quest yacht hijacking claimed the Navy and FBI's efforts to rescue the hostages led to the killings. In trials in Norfolk, Virginia, their motions stated, "The Navy's 'aggressive actions' and 'the failure to conduct the negotiations with the Somalis in a proper fashion' created an unstable situation "that resulted in the violent deaths of eight individuals."[94] The eight people mentioned included the four American hostages and two of the pirates killed by U.S. Navy SEALs during the rescue attempt.

Equally bizarre was a suit filed in Berlin on behalf of pirates captured off Somalia against the German government. Among the claims was that the German naval forces had destroyed evidence by sinking the pirate's skiff. The lawyers argued further that it was a German responsibility to ensure the pirates got a fair trial in courts in Mombasa, Kenya.[95] In addition, the lawyers wanted Germany to pay for the defense of the suspects and complained their embassy in Nairobi had not given adequate support to the case.[96]

The Problem of Boundaries

Closely entwined are the problems of borders and boundaries. They fall into three categories—geographic, administrative, and legal—and all are relatively arbitrary, yet often dealt with as if sacrosanct. They certainly impact jurisdictional issues, but also emerge for U.S. forces operating in counter-piracy missions in and near the HOA. For American forces, U.S. Africa Command (USAFRICOM) has responsibility for the continent of Africa right up to the shoreline. Once in the water, responsibility shifts to U.S. Central Command (USCENTCOM). Part of the problem is addressed by the establishment of the Combined Joint Task Force – Horn of Africa (CJTF-HOA) though they are focused on supporting the countries in eastern Africa. Created in 2009, the CJTF-HOA includes working through embassies to provide "Assistance with addressing counterterrorism, counter-piracy, and illicit trafficking."[97] It is worth noting that in addition to the U.S. there are several non-African countries participating in the CJTF-HOA including the United Kingdom, France, South Korea, Japan, and Romania.[98]

Until 2010, USAFRICOM was not involved in counter-piracy patrolling of the coast of the continent.[99] However, they were participating in activities on shore designed to build capacity and assist countries in the region to fight against the insidious criminal elements that operated from their shores. Of course, USAFRICOM is concerned with both sides of the continent. The commander, General Carter Ham stated, "Piracy and other maritime crimes negatively impact the security and freedom of access for all nations to critical waterways and continue to threaten U.S. security in the waters off the East and West coast of Africa."[100] Another addition was the positioning of the MQ-9 UAVs to assist in patrolling the vast water areas. The command announced, "The temporary stationing of MQ-9s in the Seychelles falls under the operational authority of USAFRICOM and is part of a collaborative effort of the U.S. and Seychelles governments to determine the feasibility of using UAVs in support of maritime and border-related security initiatives in and around the Indian Ocean."[101]

Once on the deep waters the counter-piracy mission transfers to the Combined Maritime Force (CMF), and Combined Task Force (CTF) 151 in

Figure 2. The guided missile destroyer USS Faragut passes by the smoke from a disabled pirate skiff. USS Faragut is part of Combined Task Force 151, a multinational task force established to conduct anti-piracy operations in the Gulf of Aden. U.S. Navy Photo by Mass Communication Specialist 1st Class Cassandra Thompson.

particular. There are two other Combined Task Forces patrolling the area with slightly different missions. CTF 150 is assigned to maritime security for Red Sea, Gulf of Aden, Indian Ocean and Gulf of Oman while CTF 152 has responsibility for maritime security in the Arabian Gulf.[102] Headquartered in Bahrain, the CMF has an even broader makeup than does Combined Joint Task Force - Horn of Africa Including the U.S. there are 26 member nations: Australia, Bahrain, Belgium, Canada, Denmark, France, Germany, Greece, Italy, Japan, Jordan, Republic of Korea, Kuwait, Malaysia, the Netherlands, New Zealand, Pakistan, Portugal, Saudi Arabia, Singapore, Spain, Thailand, Turkey, United Arab Emirates, and the United Kingdom. They are responsible for security in over 2.5 million square miles of waterways and senior staff positions are filled by officers from several countries.[103]

The impact of boundaries is recognized and was raised by General Mattis, Commander, USCENTCOM, when he reported to Congress in March 2012. In his statement he noted, "events do not occur according to the neat lines and areas of responsibility we draw on the map of the world. Security challenges posed by piracy, violent extremist organizations and criminal elements based in the HOA impact operations in the USCENTCOM AOR."[104]

In addition to the formal organizations involved in counter-piracy, another international body is the Contact Group on Piracy off the Coast of Somalia. This is an ad hoc group "not overseen or managed by any one country, but instead operates as a community of interested states with an evolving structure of working groups that report to a plenary body chaired on a rotational basis by volunteer nations. Participants also include Egypt, Japan, Greece, Norway, Korea, Turkey, and Singapore."[105]

By now the complexity of command and control issues should be apparent. But the boundary issues are deeper than just arbitrary military delineations of responsibility and the complexities of international cooperation. Country borders have their own interesting problems, including where their land begins and what constitutes territorial waters. While piracy is a universal crime and any agency can make an arrest, jurisdiction for lesser-included crimes or related issues may depend on where incidents occur.

For example, before applying for political asylum, a person must reach the land of the country receiving them. That is why definition of the shore line is important and even such trivial concerns about what constitutes reaching the beach when waves are exposing sand and then covering it back up again. This problem is frequently observed by the people from the Caribbean

Islands, especially Cubans and Haitians, fleeing their countries for Florida. The policy that has been adopted is known as "wet foot/dry foot," meaning that if refugees make it to the beach and can stand on dry land they are treated differently and acquire rights not afforded those at sea or who have "wet feet."[106] Of course, the law enforcement concept of hot pursuit is related.

> Hot pursuit may commence when the coastal state has good reason to believe that the foreign vessel has violated the state's laws and regulations and the vessel has disobeyed a clear order to stop. The chase must begin within the limits of the territorial sea or, where relevant rights have been violated, in zones further out. The right of hot pursuit ceases when the chase is interrupted or the vessel reaches the territorial sea of its own state or a third state.[107]

Whether or not a military force from third countries can pursue pirates on land may be challenged. If contact is broken and the chase not continuous, the legal definition of hot pursuit has been violated. However, from a military perspective, there may be deemed a necessity to continue the search. The lines between law enforcement requirements and operational necessity could easily become blurred. Closely associated with *hot pursuit* is the law enforcement concept of *fresh pursuit*. Fresh pursuit does not require constant observation of the fleeing suspect, but reasonable knowledge of their location. The intent is to allow police the ability to follow a suspect without stopping to get a warrant before entering a building. By policy approved by the U.S. Attorney General, fresh pursuit is defined as, "Pursuit (with or without a warrant) for the purpose of preventing the escape or effecting the arrest of any person who is suspected of committing, or having committed, a misdemeanor or felony. Fresh pursuit implies pursuit without unreasonable delay, but need not be immediate pursuit."[108]

This is an area where high technology may be able to assist. Most hot/fresh pursuit incidents assume line of sight between the pursuer and the pursued. That is one reason that police must break off a chase into another jurisdiction if they lose sight of the suspect. However, the employment of unmanned aerial vehicles may provide the continuity required to constitute continuous observation. As a minimum they will provide a different perspective and may be able to track suspects when naval surface forces cannot.

In May 2012, the EU, which had vowed to take a tougher stand against piracy in the HOA, changed the rules and took the fight to the pirates' home base. For the first time their forces attacked boats not actively engaged in an act of piracy and destroyed several of their signature fiberglass skiffs. These small boats were found on the beach in a notorious pirate-infested area of Somalia. The attack came from the air and the force did not set foot on the ground.[109] In addition to the boats, the EU naval forces also conducted an air attack against the pirate supply base destroying fuel tanks and weapons. The flames caused extensive damage to their operations as was acknowledged by a pirate leader, Bile Hussein.[110]

The attack was hailed by the military officials as taking advantage of an opportunity to hurt the pirates. It was also applauded by government officials in Somalia who had been advised of the attack beforehand, but who were unable to control their own coast. This did, however, open some new legal issues that have yet to be tested in local or international courts. From a military perspective, this seems like a logical step on counter-piracy operations. However, since piracy is being treated as a law enforcement problem, these issues of actions and boundaries remain unsettled.

There are other issues that emerge from this operation. While there were a number of the plastic-hulled skiffs used in pirate attacks that were destroyed, the helicopters also shot up several wooden dhows that are sometimes used to ferry men and goods from the ships being held hostage. However, those same boats are also used for legitimate fishing purposes and are important for providing food for the local inhabitants. Of course this is a classic problem encountered in counterinsurgency missions. Under what circumstances can the part-time support force, some of whom may be impressed, be legitimately targeted? The boarder issue here is the law enforcement model that requires proof in a court of law, versus a military model of attacking a potential threat.

The raid conducted by European forces exemplifies the divisions in thinking that emerged in their debate about changing the rules of use of force. It is reported that France, the Netherlands, and the United Kingdom wanted to deny pirates sanctuary by following them on land. Germany, Austria, and Spain were not anxious to go along over concern of casualties on all sides. The compromise was that helicopters could be used, but no troops on the ground. The agreement also raised boundaries issues such as: How wide is a beach? How far can pirates be tracked on internal waterways? What weapons are authorized? The decision was that machineguns were permissible, but not rockets. Even "who is a pirate" might be questioned since they sometimes employ private citizens for support.[111]

6. Costs of Piracy

There are many costs associated with piracy. While ever increasing ransom demands attract media attention, they are only a small fraction of the estimated $7 billion annual price tag. In fact, ransom account for only about 2 percent of the bill. While the number of successful pirate attacks recently has declined, the total costs continue to rise. The significant factors in avoiding pirate takeovers at sea are increasing speed of cargo vessels and additional security measures.

By increasing cruising speed, especially of the larger ships, it has become more difficult for the small pirate boats to come alongside and board their target. So far, no ship traveling faster than 18 knots has been successfully captured. However, by traveling faster, these vessels dramatically increase the cost of fuel consumed. It is estimated that this tactic accounts for about 40 percent of the costs associated with piracy. In 2011, additional fuel costs to avoid pirates amounted to approximately $2.7 billion. That is true even though the speeds are increased only in high-risk areas.[112] There is another $600 million in additional costs for simply rerouting ships for greater distances and avoiding the danger zone altogether.

As can be expected, insurance companies have increased their fees as well. The price tag for covering ships entering the area is over $600 million. The insurance companies consider the waters off Somalia to be a "war risk" and can thus inflate the costs. Some insurers have added a "pirate surcharge" of a reported $20,000 per trip.[113] They also sell kidnap and ransom insurance to cover recovery efforts if crew members are taken hostage. This is quite a lucrative sector for the insurance industry, even if they have to pay an occasional ransom. The profit margin is over 300 percent of what they pay out. As seen in the examples provided earlier, the insurance negotiators have been very successful in convincing the pirates, or their representatives, to lower their demands to a small fraction of the original requirement.

The second most significant factor in avoiding hijacking at sea is the addition of private security personnel. Since these are not seamen assigned to the tasks of running the ship, they constitute a financial burden. It is estimated that about 25 percent of the ships transiting the Gulf of Aden now carry armed guards. Some of the weapons available to them will be discussed shortly. The cost per ship per voyage to have an armed security detail runs about $40,000 to 60,000.[114] It is noted that having armed guards on board can decrease some of the insurance premiums.[115] Since they are operating in dangerous areas, payroll costs also increase as bonuses are required to entice crews to join on risky ventures. While not a great amount in the overall scheme of counter-piracy, the payroll increase is about equal to the amount paid out in ransom demands.

It is not just seamen who are involved in negotiating costs, such as pay for high risk travel. Recently their families have entered the equation via the legal system. Family members have sued some shipping companies that have experienced hijackings for knowingly putting their employees at risk. These actions have also led to demands from family members that owners hire ship riders to protect their crews. Their threat is that if crew personnel are captured, the companies will be sued for large sums of money. A cost-benefit analysis would suggest it is cheaper to hire guards than litigate against substantial payoffs in court.[116]

In addition to the costs borne by private companies, governments also pay a considerable amount for piracy. More than 30 countries are now engaged in counter-piracy operations. The estimated combined budget for such operations was about $1.3 billion. It must also be taken into account the missions these navies did not accomplish because they were tied up chasing ghosts.

As noted earlier, there are expenses related to the trials and incarceration of pirates. While this is a stumbling block for poor countries in the region, the amount paid for these services is extremely modest. For 2011, it was estimated that prosecution costs were only $16.4 million, or less than two tenths of one percent of the total lost to piracy. As indicated above, governments spend well over a billion dollars to support navies tracking the pirates, yet spend a miniscule amount to cover the costs once they are captured. The impact is both clear and frustrating. Many of the captured pirates simply go free in a relatively short period of time. Jack Lang, UN Special Adviser on Piracy, estimated that the number released without charges at over 90 percent of those arrested.[117] It is not uncommon for them to return to their lucrative trade.

In addition to money, there are human costs associated with piracy. For several years, hostages held captive had an excellent chance of survival. Worth more alive than dead, the pirates took steps to insure they could deliver them when the ransom was paid. It was a good business model to keep up their end of the bargain with an eye on negotiations in future operations. There have been recent changes in the negotiation for release of hostages. Sometimes a few of the hostages are kept back by the pirates to be exchanged for their compatriots who are being held for trial. While most pirates are released without trial, this process is designed to free the ones remaining in legal custody.

However, in recent years the probability of fatal consequences has increased and raised fears that pirates are becoming more violent. In 2008, only four hostages died in the hands of pirates, while in 2011 that number had risen to 24. It is also noted that hostages are being held for longer periods of time, often many months before being released. The average time in captivity was up to five months and the longest, M/V Iceberg 1, was two years and nine months.[118]

Reports also link other human costs. Of those taken hostage, at least 60 percent were either used as human shields or physically abused by their captors—in some cases, both occurred. Although kept alive, the physical conditions in which they are held is rather poor. There are also long-term psychological effects on the seafarers and their families.[119]

Ransom Issues

The payment of ransom is very controversial. It is still a common practice, however, and the existing laws and regulations may actually complicate the situation. Those laws vary from country to country, and U.S. policy is to make no concessions to pirates and kidnappers. There are several justifications for assuming that position. One of the most prominent is the assumption that payment of ransom to a kidnapper will encourage other criminals to follow that model.[120] There is considerable evidence that such rationale is valid. Certainly piracy in the HOA increased as the criminals seemed to be rewarded, often handsomely, for their ventures. Whether or not criminalization of ransom payments would deter wannabe pirates is an untested theory, but still postulated. Another serious concern is that the ransom is used to finance other crime and terrorism. This too has established validity. The arguments supporting criminalization are supported by a purely logical and dispassionate standpoint. They run counter to the emotional pleas when actually confronted with real human beings held under constant threats of death. It also must be acknowledged that in most cases, the payment of ransom results in the release of the person or persons held hostage. For the kidnapping process to continue to work successfully, it is generally in the best interests of the criminals to insure safe return of their hostages once they have been paid.

Under U.S. law, it appears that payment of ransom is illegal. On 13 April 2010, President Obama signed an Executive Order that was designed to counter piracy in the HOA area.[121] Broad in nature, the executive order laid out a number of prohibitions for providing support to pirates or terrorists. One subparagraph states, "The prohibitions in subsection (a) of this section include but are not limited to: (i) the making of any contribution or provision of funds, goods, or services by, to, or for the benefit of any person whose property and interests in property are blocked pursuant to this order; and (ii) the receipt of any contribution or provision of funds, goods, or services from any such person."

Under U.S. law, it appears that payment of ransom is illegal.

This has been interpreted to mean that any payment of ransom to pirates would be construed as providing illegal support to terrorists. There are draconian consequences that may follow, including the obvious freezing of funds held in U.S. financial institutions. It may also mean that specific ships, or companies owning ships and have paid ransom, may be barred from entering American ports. As might be expected, companies and pirates have been working around these restrictions. From an American perspective, the law only allows forfeiture of funds if a U.S. citizen is involved in the ransom transactions. The obvious solution is that only people from third countries be included in negotiations. British law, for example, does allow the payment of ransom as a logical means to preserve life. Another circumvention of intent is the misidentification of money for other purposes. Providing humanitarian aid, versus ransom, has been mentioned as a possible ploy for moving large sums of money.

In Somalia it is, however, illegal to pay ransom. That appears to be the reason that a preferred method of delivery of money is by parachute onto the beleaguered ship. Other means of direct payments have been attempted. In the case of the hijacking of the Chinese vessel MV Yuan Xiang and East African risk-management company, Salama Fikira moved $3.6M from the Seychelles to Mogadishu. The intent was to place the cash on a smaller aircraft and then to be dropped to the pirates. However, the shipment was confiscated by airport security and three Britons, two Kenyans and an American were arrested, charged, and sentenced to jail. They were subsequently pardoned by the President of Somalia, but the government kept the money.[122] The French government also has a policy to never pay ransom to pirates and kidnappers. In the case previously covered of the sailing ship Le Pocant, the news release specifically stated that "no public money was paid." Obviously they were splitting hairs and the money came allegedly from the shipping company, not government coffers. The company declined to comment.[123]

There are established relationships between piracy for ransom and kidnap for ransom yet they are considered separate categories of crime and both are used as means to finance terrorism.[124] In particular, it is reported that significant amounts of ransom payments to Somali pirates is funneled to al-Shabaab which has increasingly strong ties to al-Qaeda. The official acknowledgment of such connections between pirates and designated terrorists organizations clearly would make ransom payments to HOA pirates illegal under any circumstance.[125]

Further complicating decisions regarding whether ransom payments should be made are the insurance companies with policies covering the ships taken by pirates. In some cases they recognize that it would be more cost effective to pay ransom and retrieve the cargo. This was borne out by a claim to recover insurance when the *Bunga Melati Dua* was captured. Though acknowledging the issue of undesirability to public interest, the court found "that payment of a ransom reflected strong likelihood that payment of a ransom would secure recovery of both, the vessel and the cargo."[126] Thus, the value of the insurance payment was diminished. Such rulings put shipping companies in the most difficult position of having to choose between obeying legal restrictions with limited consequences, and economic realities that suggest paying ransom is an efficacious business decision.

Because of the legal issues surrounding the payment of ransom, those involved, including financial institutions, insurance companies, and shipping companies, are loath to acknowledge their actions and evade reporting requirements.

> Once ransoms are paid and the cash subsequently enters Somalia, 'following the money' becomes difficult because there are no mechanisms to identify the source and destination of these funds and because the trail goes cold if such payments were not previously

reported to FIUs (financial intelligence units) and other AML/CFT (anti-money laundering/counter-terror financing) authorities.[127]

There is considerable cooperation between law enforcement agencies regarding financial crimes and money laundering. The large amount of cash paid in ransom transactions affords a vulnerability to the pirate organizations if they use traditional financial institutions to move money. Gaining sophistication, more experienced organizations have learned how to hide funds in institutions not complying with international reporting regulations. These are usually located in countries not directly involved with the piracy operations yet have links to groups that support terrorism or organized crime. One successful alternative method of moving funds has been the adaption of the age old Hawala systems that rely on personal contacts and family/tribal loyalties.[128] In addition, substantial amounts of money are moved by cash couriers. The couriers are vulnerable to interception by law enforcement agencies. There are practical limits as to how much can be carried by any individual, even when large bills are involved. Movement of tens of thousands of dollars to support terrorist activities has been repeatedly demonstrated.[129] Confiscation of large amounts of cash that is unaccounted for in any system is a tempting enticement for corruption. As with the vast sums expropriated with drug smuggling, ransom recovery presents extreme ethical challenges for all involved.

7. Self Defense Mechanisms

There are tough questions raised when considering appropriate levels of defense for commercial vessels, and these intersect directly with special operations missions. One such example was the taking and later freeing of the Italian-flagged ship MV Montecristo. On 10 October 2011, with security guards unarmed, the crews dashed for a safe room and sent out a distress call. Firing only one shot, the pirates quickly scrambled onto the ship, only to find the crew maintained control of the engine room and were steering the vessel in circles. In this case, NATO Task Force Operation Ocean Shield was able to respond in a timely manner. With the crew safely accounted for, special operations elements were deployed onto the ship capturing 11 pirates who surrendered rather than fight a well-armed maritime military force.[130] The rescue was a combined effort with U.S. and United Kingdom forces involved.

There have been many studies that have made a variety of recommendations for countering piracy. These include efforts taken by the maritime shipping industry to better safeguard their vessels, commitment of international naval forces, intervention by international financial crimes organizations, and building capacity in African countries most impacted by piracy. The latter effort is very broad and may include enhancing governance, legal structures, and economic situations. These actions sound very much like nation building, and are very controversial given the current economic situations across the globe.

For self-protection, most large commercial vessels have automated alert systems, like bank panic buttons. It has been proposed that this capability be installed on larger fishing boats and trawlers as well.[131] Pirates take note of which ships have active protection and even which companies are known to pay ransom. They are more likely to attack ships of companies that have previously paid them. Given the vastness of the seas, alarms do not guarantee the cavalry will arrive and save them, but it greatly improves their chances of rescue.

Today many ships have a secure area to which the crew can retreat when threatened by pirates. They have proven effective in several such as the Magellan Star, Maersk Alabama, Montecristo, and an unnamed Greek oil tanker attacked off Nigeria in June 2012. To be successful, it is important that adequate training be provided so their use is understood by all members of the crew. Drills should be conducted before entering high-risk areas. The designated safe areas must be provisioned with adequate food and water, have effective communications and navigation capabilities, and proper sanitation that allows the crew to remain safe for several days.[132]

Planning is an essential part of all counter-piracy efforts. Among the tools available is a chart compiled by the Hydrographic Office of the United Kingdom regarding the Gulf of Aden, the Red Sea, and the Arabian Sea. It advises sailors with detailed description of voluntary reporting requirements, navigation in or near pirate high-risk areas, and actions to be taken in the event of a suspected or actual pirate attack.[133] Staying away from pirates, while more difficult now that they are supported by mother ships, is one of the best methods to avoid capture. There is fuel cost versus time and distance trade off, and a risk-benefit analysis must be made by each captain. In the case of the Maersk Alabama hijacking, the crew later complained that Captain Phillips had taken unnecessary risks by steering a short course to Mombasa. They filed suit claiming "the companies ignored warnings about Somali pirates and sailed too close to the Somali coast."[134]

For ships transiting their area of responsibility, there are several of common sense self-protective measures that are recommended by CTF-151. They state:

> Advice and guidance on avoiding piracy and is targeted at seafarers who intend to travel through the Gulf of Aden, Somali Basin and the Indian Ocean. Measures include: maintaining a proactive 24 hour lookout; reporting suspicious activities to authorities; removing access ladders; protecting the lowest points of access; the use of deck lighting, netting, razor wire, electrical fencing, fire hoses and surveillance and detection equipment; engaging in evasive maneuvering and speed during a pirate attacks; and joining group transits.[135]

In an extraordinary move, military forces came together to support the film industry to provide a documentary to inform the shipping companies and the public about the perils of piracy and protective measures. Produced in 2012 and titled, *Piracy – Menace at Sea* it is now available to the public.[136]

Vessels sailing in the area impacted by piracy have implemented several defensive mechanisms to enhance their safety. One simple approach for larger ships is to increase speed of travel. It is noted that ships traveling less than 16 knots are at much higher risk, especially if they have a low freeboard. At slower speeds, the smaller boats operated by pirates can easily come alongside and board the craft while maintaining comparable speed.[137] The downside to this countermeasure is a significant increase in fuel costs for running at higher speed.

Ships that cannot outrun pirates are recommended to engage in maneuvering away from attackers and frequent course changes. When the smaller craft are operating very close to their targets, they are sometimes subject to being swamped. Several pirate vessels have been sunk by this response. Such was the case of the Maersk Alabama, but led to another problem—namely the pirates who had already boarded had no way to leave the ship. The frequent change of course must be consistent with safe navigation practices and take into account other merchant ships transiting the area.

Active defense measures have been controversial. In general, seamen are not trained in basic military skills. Simply providing them weapons is insufficient and potentially dangerous. There is nothing worse than an untrained person operating firearms. Many ships are reluctant to have deadly weapons on board, and national laws can be problematic. Many countries have laws prohibiting the import of any firearms. These laws may not discriminate between those smuggling in weapons and ships carrying a few weapons for self defense. The general rule is no tolerance. Obviously weapons smuggling is an art that is widely practiced with considerable success.

Some companies have begun employing private security firms with highly trained counter-piracy personnel. Under some circumstances they can be very effective. They do add costs to the company and detract from the profit margin. Like carrying weapons, private security forces have legal liabilities as well. Most countries require licensing of these privately armed agents, but there are multijurisdictional problems as well. How they operate on the high seas is one of them, especially if they employ deadly force.

Ship Riders

One of the most controversial yet effective counter-piracy measures is the use of armed guards, sometimes known as ship riders. While this approach may seem intuitively obvious, it is fraught with legal and bureaucratic issues. A most important issue is that there are no international standards either on the high seas or in nationally controlled territory. For clarification, this section does not refer to the U.S. Navy program for inter-navy cooperation and training that also calls participants ship riders.[138]

Worth noting is that protective ship riders may either be law enforcement personnel assigned to vessels to expedite arrest procedures or private security guards with no powers of arrest. In a legal sense, law enforcement personnel acting as ship riders usually are on board to assist in a specific mission, such as counter-narcotics, stem illegal immigration, or even prevent fishing violations. The broader context, which is described here, includes the use of armed guards for the purpose of stopping pirates from boarding their craft.

So far those providing armed support have been successful in that no ship so equipped had been successfully boarded. For private security companies, providing support to ocean-going vessels is a growth market. There are many companies from several countries now participating in counter-piracy operations. There is also wide variability in the capabilities they provide, but it is indicated that with increased use of ship riders, the number of violent encounters has gone up.[139] By December of 2012, it was estimated that 60 percent of commercial ships employed armed private security guards. They have contributed to a significant decrease in successful pirate attacks albeit at significant added expense.[140]

Until recently, extending the route often was a viable option for avoiding pirates. While that increased fuel charges, it did ensure safety of the crew and cargo. However, with the advent of more capable mother-ships, there is nowhere in the region between African and India to avoid them. Therefore, shipping companies must make difficult decisions about the most cost-effective methods for countering piracy.

There are several U.S.-based companies that provide armed escorts.[141] Senior personnel indicate that working with the DOS and attempting to comply with all of the hurdles they impose is draconian. In addition, the rules and regulations vary with every country involved. While there are always ways to get around regulations, it is considered dangerous, and unethical, to do so. There are many foreign-owned companies that also offer armed security protection for ships transiting dangerous waters. While they face other bureaucratic entanglements, they are not restricted by American arms export regulations.

A fundamental problem is the international transport and possession of firearms. There are a number of countries that will not allow ships carrying basic weapons, such as rifles and pistols, from entering their waters or ports.

Thus, moving arms and people to guard the vessels can be a very complicated problem. American companies involved in ship security also must be compliant with the many constraints imposed by the DOS International Trade in Arms Regulation (ITAR).[142]

To circumvent such issues, there are now commercial ventures established to address the arms smuggling conundrum. There are now about 20 ships serving as floating arsenals located in the Gulf of Aden, the Red Sea, and Indian Ocean regions.[143] These ships hold small arms and ammunition while ships proceed to their destination. Their mission is to meet ships destined for local ports and offload the weapons in international waters just prior to arrival. The weapons are then returned to crews of outbound vessels. The legal status of floating arsenals has yet to be determined. Lacking standards, some of these arsenals may provide tempting targets for the pirates.[144] Another less desirable approach has been to simply dump the weapons overboard before entering restricted waters. For those using expensive sniper rifles, this can be an expensive, but legally safe, option.[145]

Another serious consideration is the consequences of use of force, especially deadly force. All ships have the right to protect themselves from pirates. However, the rules for reporting incidents and providing assistance to pirates in disabled boats vary depending on the relative position of employment one holds on the ship at the time of the attack. It was reported that ship riders can use deadly force to repulse pirates and are not required to even report the incident.[146] If the pirate's boats become disabled during their assault the guards have no further responsibility. However, the ship's captain may be in a very different situation. The laws of the sea require that the same vessel provide assistance to any craft that is disabled. These laws, designed to aid legitimately distressed sailors and fishermen, did not envision circumstances in which a captain may be obligated to come to the aid of a group that immediately preceding their demise had been actively engaged in hostile criminal activity and attempting to capture them.

Determining which approaching boats contain pirates and those that are innocent fishing vessels can be difficult. Mistakes can be costly. In February 2012, civilian Italian marines who were guarding an oil tanker opened fire on an unarmed trawler killing two Indian fishermen. The MV Enrica Lexie was at anchor off the port of Kochi when the mistaken identity occurred. The marines claimed self-defense as the guards believed that their ship was about to be boarded. In response, the Indian government opened a murder investigation.[147] The investigation noted that the trawler was 100 meters from the Enrica Lexie when the shooting took place, and those who died had been sleeping at the time of the incident.

This incident also highlighted the legal problems that confront ship riders. Brought into the negotiations was the Italian foreign ministry which objected to the marines being tried under Indian jurisprudence and in attempted to gain their release on bail. Their argument was that since the marines were engaged in counter-piracy, under international agreement they should have immunity. However, the Indian government disagreed, denied bail, and continued with the prosecution.[148]

There is considerable sensitivity surrounding all aspects of this controversy. As an example, the term "rules of engagement" was believed by some in the shipping industry to sound too military-like. The International Maritime preferred "rules on use of force." There is even distinction drawn between counter-piracy, as a law enforcement issue, versus when force is used in self-protection. The problems were well stated as, "The distinction between maritime law enforcement and the use of force at sea is as intricate in law as it is fundamental in practice. Many international legal aspects regarding the determination of the nature of forcible measures against foreign ships at sea have remained largely unexplored."[149] Others have noted that the laws as currently configured are inadequate to deal with piracy in general, and that certainly applies to the actions of ship riders in armed interventions against pirates.[150]

Trident Group president, Tom Rothrauff, a former SEAL, emphasized that maritime security is quite different from safeguarding people and facilities on land. He noted that you cannot just hire individuals who are trained to shoot and expect them to operate effectively in the complex situations found at sea. The concern is that companies will hire private security guards that have never operated in a maritime environment. The private security industry already suffers from negative images derived from shooting incidents in Iraq. As a cost-saving measure, many companies resorted to hiring former military personnel from third world countries, or reduced their standards for others. Such practices will likely lead to more unfortunate incidents on the high seas, and influence the adaptations of laws and regulations.[151]

Typically there are four to six men employed to guard a vessel. Since they are rarely merchant sailors, guard duty and related drills are their sole functions while on board. One of the bureaucratic issues that have arisen is whether or not these guards are required to have seaman's paper. According to U.S. law merchant seamen who are unlicensed are required to have a valid Merchant Mariner's Document if they are serving on an American vessel. There is an established hierarchy of qualifications, but none would seem to fit these duties.

Ship riders operate independently as small teams. Unlike their naval counterparts, there is little, if any, backup force available should a situation develop that they cannot handle. Since the shipping industry often operates on an unscheduled basis, their tour of duty may change abruptly. Guards have boarded ships expecting the transit to take only a few days, and yet not terminated their trip for several weeks. Others have entered for a long haul and completed their task in less than a week.[152]

> *Ship riders operate independently as small teams. Unlike their naval counterparts, there is little, if any, backup force available should a situation develop that they cannot handle.*

Targeting cruise ships has become a topic of concern and one that may be related to ship riders. While there have been some brief encounters between pirates and cruise ships, many experts do not think they are likely to be taken for purposes of ransom. The basic problem would be controlling large numbers of people. The logistics would be extremely complex and very hard for a pirate crew to manage. Very few pirates are really experienced, let alone educated well enough for such an undertaking. Cognizant of the potential threat, cruise ships employ maritime intelligence services and receive frequent updates of pirate activity anywhere close to their location.[153]

However, cruise ships were among the targets being considered by Osama bin Laden and al-Qaeda.[154] Rather than traditional piracy, the intent of such attacks would be for terrorism. Also, they were considering ships in European waters, thus attracting world attention. It was mentioned that hostages could be traded for political prisoners, but that executions would likely be necessary as a demonstration of resolve. Details included dressing hostages in orange uniforms "as if they were al Qaeda prisoners at Guantanamo Bay."[155] As with American journalist Daniel Pearl[156] and other unfortunate victims, the executions would be recorded and made available on the Internet for maximum psychological effect.

The cruise industry does take the potential of a terrorist attack quite seriously. One issue is the diverse population of both passengers and the crew. It is not uncommon to have representation of more than 50 countries on any one ship at any given time. Not all of those countries have friendly relationships, a concern already noted by cruise lines. Checking for obvious weapons, all luggage is normally x-rayed before being taken aboard. Passengers generally are required to go through metal detectors and their hand carried items screened as well. There are concerns, however, that components of weapons or materials for explosives can be dispersed and hidden in such a manner that they are not detectable by routine security means. Unlike on aircraft, passengers have complete access to their luggage and would have days to assemble weapons or make bombs. The security personnel on board cruise ships usually are not armed. The thinking is that having any weapons increases the danger to passengers and crew.[157] Therefore, any terrorist with a weapon would have a significant advantage in use of force. While SOF intervention in countering a terrorist attack on a cruise ship is beyond the scope of this monograph, it is noted as the considerations would be far more complex than retaking a cargo vessel.

That concept is not without precedence. During the hijacking of the MS Achille Lauro off of Egypt on 7 October 1985, in an aggressive and unanticipated move it took only four members of the Palestine Liberation Front to wrest control of the ship with over 400 passengers and crew. Their demand was the release of Palestinian prisoners being held in Israel. To emphasize their demand, the terrorists shot a disabled American passenger, Leon Klinghoffer, and threw his body and wheelchair overboard.[158]

This case is emblazoned on the annals of SOF history as counter-terror units were brought into action. It also demonstrated the international problems associated with such actions when a plane carrying Abu Abbas and the hijackers was intercepted by the U.S. Air Force and forced down in Sigonella, Sicily and Italian officials wanted to maintain jurisdiction rather than allowing the American forces to arrest them for the murder of Klinghoffer. A full description of that interaction can be found in former USSOCOM commander, General Carl Stiner's account in his book *Shadow Warriors*.[159]

The Achille Lauro precedent demonstrates that a small number of terrorists can quickly capture a cruise ship. While most lines have some level of security on board, they are oriented toward small community policing, not criminals armed with automatic weapons. As a cost-saving measure, the guards themselves are often from Third World countries but are not armed. Work in this image-conscious industry is intent on making passengers forget about the concerns of the external world except when absolutely necessary. Behind the scenes senior leadership is aware of potential threats to cruise ships and view that threat as more terrorism than piracy. However, when transiting seas known for piracy, passengers are provided written notification of the potential threat and the actions that will be taken in the event of an attack. They are told that the captain will announce the emergency as the ship increases speed. They will initiate zigzag maneuvers in and attempt swamp the pirates. Passengers are therefore informed to stay away from windows, make their way to the center of the ship and lie down. In the event of being boarded by pirates they are to offer no resistance.[160] The counter-piracy training for the crew is focused on them keeping passengers as calm as possible.[161] It would appear that the next market for combat trained ship riders may well be the cruise industry.

As the maritime protection industry continues to grow, recruitment and retention of trained personnel could become an issue. Just as private security companies during Operation Iraqi Freedom attracted some well-qualified SOF personnel, there is a potential for current members to join these services. At present the U.S. companies involved in providing ship riders only take applications from people who have retired or otherwise completed their period of enlistment.[162] While recruiting and retention is not a current problem, the trend is worth watching.

There are critical decisions that need to be made when vessels determine that they will take active measures against pirates. Some advice has been made available in maritime channels in gradually escalating responses to the threat. The rules in use of force in piracy attacks dictate clear identification and warning by the vessel being attacked that it has deadly force capability. Use of systems such as the Long Range Acoustic Device (LRAD) provides that capability, but simply showing arms may be sufficient. Before shooting at an intruder, their hostile intent must be clearly identified. For later legal purposes, it is best that visual and audio recording equipment be used to document the activity. The pirates should be warned off repeatedly with all communications means available including radio, loud hailers, and even bright lights if available.

If warnings are ignored, it is suggested that weapons fire should be directed near, but not directly at, the attacking vessel in an attempt to turn back or ward off the attack. If the attacking vessel does not turn away, a vessel-disabling barrage may be next mounted in order to avoid loss of human life. Note this may be more difficult than the theoreticians conceptualize since the actions may be taken by sailors with limited, or no combat experience. At this point in escalation of force, personnel trained in marine warfare are best suited. As a final step and when dissuasion fails to turn the pirates away and they continue to close in and maintain the attack, use of deadly force is necessary.[163]

Nonlethal Weapons Alternatives

Most recommendations for active defensive measures call for nonlethal weapons. There are a number of such systems now available and some have been used with varying success. One of the better-known types of weapons is acoustic in nature. These acoustic weapons have many advantages. First, they are highly directional. Early attempts at employ sound were omnidirectional, meaning everyone was exposed to the noise. Current systems project a beam that is narrowly focused and only a few degrees wide. Technically they are directed energy weapons, but without the emotional baggage of high-power microwaves or lasers.

One problem facing ships experiencing small boats approaching has been determining intent. The tragic case that exemplifies that issue was the 12 October 2000 bombing of the USS Cole while docked at a port in Yemen. In that case the terrorists came immediately along-side with the captain waving and smiling at the Navy personnel in sight. It was not until he detonated the bomb, killing 17 U.S. Navy personnel and wounding another 39, that his intent was known.[164] As a result of this incident, the U.S. Navy requested a study of non-lethal weapon alternatives by the National Research Council which provided a catalogue of possible technologies.[165]

In addition to physical barriers, acoustic devices allow the broadcast of messages to any approaching boat. The volume is sufficiently loud as to insure that will be heard unless the operator is wearing hearing protection. The sound quality is amazingly clear and thus it can be assumed that people on board the targeted boat have received a warning and continued movement infers intent. The system allows for the volume to be increased to levels that can induce pain. While countermeasures are available, most people exposed to that intensity will divert.

The LRAD is such a non-lethal system that has received considerable press.[166] On 5 November 2005 the passenger cruise ship, *Seabourn Spirit*, was attacked by pirates 115 kilometer off the coast of Somalia. Despite being fired on with machineguns and RPGs by the attackers, the crew used the LRAD to keep them at bay. The encounter was not entirely nonlethal, as the captain of the cruise liner managed to run over one of the speed boats. Still, this event confirmed the effectiveness of LRAD.[167] There are several acoustic systems available on the open market. When traveling in the Gulf of Guinea, the Silver Wind placed a Magnetic Audio Device (MAD) on the stern of the ship and substantially increased surveillance on the ship.[168] With amazing clarity and, audible ranges in excess of a mile, the MAD is designed primarily as a warning mechanism to let approaching vessels know they have been spotted. That is sometimes sufficient to dissuade pirates from attacking. However, the device can be used as a weapon by projecting extremely loud, piecing sound.[169] When long range acoustic systems are employed there should be no doubt that the warning has been delivered. Ignoring such a warning can be taken as intent and escalation of force recommended.

Another popular and simple anti-piracy nonlethal weapon is use of water. All large ships have hoses on board for fighting fires, so this is a no additional cost option. The pressure coming out of the fire hose nozzles is typically 650 to 800 pounds per square inch with bursts at even higher impact. Such a stream of water is sufficient to serve as a weapon against pirates attempting to clamor up the sides using rope ladders. However, there are sometimes problems with getting the hoses to the location of the attempted boarding as the design was for fighting fires on board the

Figure 3. Ship's Serviceman 1st Class Scott D. Amberger aims a Long Range Acoustic Device at an incoming small craft off the starboard bridge wing of amphibious command ship USS Blue Ridge during a small boat attack drill. U.S. Navy photo.

vessel. Another concern is exposing the crew to small arms fire from the attackers. There have been some recent innovations in development of water cannons. That includes high pressure systems that are installed at locations of potential boarding that are remotely controlled. That eliminates the risk of injury to crew members as no one has to be present.

Light is also effective as nonlethal weapons. The simplest forms are extremely bright conventional lights that prevent an attacker from acquiring their target. They are most effective at night, and that is when a large number of raids have occurred. Some of the models available are powerful enough to be effective in daylight hours as well. The addition of strobe light mechanisms can increase their deterrent value. These systems often dazzle attackers, but will not cause any permanent damage to their eyes.

Columned light beams in the form of laser weapons can also be employed. These may or may not be nonlethal depending on the power levels available. High-power lasers could actually cut holes in an attacker's boat and sink it. While the U.S. Navy is more interested in an anti-missile laser defense, they have demonstrated the ability to disable small craft engines using them.[170]

The use of lasers on the battlefield has also proven to be an effective deterrent. Even technologically unsophisticated adversaries understand what the red dot on the chest means—that you have been targeted by a far more powerful weapon, and failure to comply likely means death. There have been recorded incidents in which terrorists have surrendered just knowing that their location has been so identified.

One big advantage lasers have is their speed-of-light delivery. The downside to lasers is that they require power to operate. While power sources have become more compact, they still take up room. In the National Research Council's nonlethal weapons study for the U.S. Navy, it was discovered that even for the addition of new, important capabilities, commanders were loath to relinquish precious space. Worth noting is the considerable research and development that has gone into airborne laser weapons. They have overcome one of the big obstacles of thermal blooming through use of adaptive optics. That was extremely important for operating lasers near sea level and dramatically increased the range capabilities for lasers. While placing lasers on many ships may be impractical, providing an airborne capability that can cover a wide area may afford great advantages in a counter-piracy role.[171]

An emerging weapon that has been discussed for several missions including counter-piracy is the Active Denial System (ADS). Unfortunately, this has acquired the popular moniker "Pain Ray" by the media. The ADS is a millimeter wave beam weapon that has been under development for decades. It was first publicly revealed in 2001 and has had a number of "unveilings" as successive news organizations discover it. A truly nonlethal weapon, it was developed to provide troops significant standoff distance when confronted by rioters. The desire was to have a system that was "better than a rock," meaning having a range exceeding 60 meters.

Operating at about 95 gigahertz, the beam has limited penetration of the skin, only a few millimeters, but does quickly engage the pain receptors and creates the sensation of heat. The ADS is extremely safe to operate, has had very few injuries associated with it, and no long-term adverse effects have been noted. Most important is that the pain stops instantly when the subject moves outside the narrowly focused beam. The weapon is effective at ranges over a kilometer.[172]

The ADS was one of the options considered during the National Research Council study of possible nonlethal weapons for ship defense in response to the bombing of the USS Cole. While advances have been made, size and cost are still drawbacks. Both are coming down, and a civilian model, Silent Guardian, is being made available, albeit with shorter range. About one third the size of the ADS, this model trades size for range.[173] The effects are rapid and compelling.

8. Role of the Military in Counter-Piracy

Piracy and maritime irregular warfare have been confronted by the U.S. Navy since its inception. Their battles have not just been on the high seas, but also in the littorals and on land as well. These engagements preferentially are now termed *confronting irregular warfare*, a broader term that eliminates some of the definitional boundaries endemic to these topics.[174] The Navy's vision statement on the subject outlines their goals:

- Enhance and formalize interoperability with U.S. government, public and private organizations, allied maritime and land forces, and regional allies
- Build partner capacity by forming enduring trust-based relationships, promoting shared interests in collective security, and providing training and resources to enhance indigenous security force capacity
- Improve our regional awareness and understanding of complex environments and challenges through intelligence and information systems, training, education, and more culturally adept approaches
- Achieve an improved understanding ability to counter illicit and extremist actors as they leverage and maneuver in their maritime and shore environments
- Enhance and broaden the multi-mission capabilities and applications of today's force to maximize effectiveness in complex regions and scenarios
- Identify necessary and distinct shifts in emphasis and investment to confront irregular challenges to include modifications to training, doctrine, and existing forces, and where necessary, new investments in processes, platforms, and systems[175]

Well stated and comprehensive, many of those missions traditionally reside within SOF. Assuming this statement is meant to be inclusive, SOF naval elements would be integrally involved in implementation of most aspects of the plan. For SOF operators who may engage in retaking a ship that has been hijacked, it would be useful to know what the crew has been instructed to do in that eventuality. In fact, maritime publications have established standardized procedures for what to do before and during a pirate attack, as well as actions during a military intervention. Preparation begins with keen observation so the crew is not surprised by the pirates. If attacked, captains are advised to go full speed and maneuver away from the small boats while creating as much wash as possible in an attempt to swamp them. They recommend activating nonlethal defensive measures such as water sprays while the remainder of the crew heads for a citadel (if available).[176]

If pirates successfully board the ship, the crew is advised to not offer any resistance on the bridge but to stop the main engine and activate emergency signal and tracking devices including the Automatic Identification and the Ship Security Alert System which alerts security personnel abroad to the situation. The manual warns that pirates may be high on drugs. If possible, have crew members in the citadel take over control of the engines and steering.[177]

Importantly, the crew members of large ships probably have been instructed on their actions in the event that a rescue force arrives on the ship. Specifically they are told: cover their head with both hands and keep them visible; make no movement that can be misinterpreted as aggressive; use no flash photography; and be prepared to be challenged on their identification.[178]

While English may be understood by many mariners, it is not universal. Instructions to crew members include the likelihood of problems with languages and interpretation of verbal commands. Given that the crew may come from different countries, this can be a significant issue. Also, the multinational nature of counter-piracy military task forces may complicate communications.

The Strategic Question: How important is counter-piracy to National Security?

The view of the importance of counter-piracy operations varies widely, even among experts. Most news media would have the public believe it is a high-priority issue. Dramatic cases with video coverage do make exciting stories and attract attention. The reality is that only a few of the cases mentioned have significant impact on the public. Of direct concern to the U.S. Department of Defense is the amount of resources that can be relegated to counter-piracy operations. It is important to acknowledge that the naval commitment in the Middle East is a considerable portion of the total U.S. fleet. However, while missions to keep the sea lanes open may include engaging pirates that interfere with cargo vessels, they constitute a tiny fraction of the current threat.

The main focus for the near term is keeping the Strait of Hormuz open. The near-constant threat to the area posed by adversarial relations with Iran demand omnipresent vigilance. These straits constrain the flow of oil from many of the Gulf States and alternatives such as constructing long pipelines do not meet the demand. It is estimated that 3,000 ships per day and 40 percent of the total traded oil supply passes through this relatively confined body of water. Mere hiccups in international relations have immediate and dramatic impact on energy prices around the world.[179]

In addition to transport issues, the threat that Iran may develop a nuclear weapon requires considerable attention. The United States has gone on record drawing a proverbial line in the sand stating no nuclear weapons will be allowed in the area and that we are prepared to exercise military force, if necessary, to prevent that from happening. According to former Secretary of State Hillary Clinton, "Washington is committed to preventing Iran from having the capability to make nuclear weapons, not only from their actual construction."[180]

As a side note, it was ironic that despite the tensions between the U.S. and Iran, when their commercial ships were captured by pirates, it was the U.S. Navy that rescued the crew. In January 2012, 13 fishermen that had been held for 40 days were saved. The official response from Iran was quite muted.[181]

It should be obvious that these strategic missions are much higher priorities than any counter-piracy efforts. The resources available in the region are finite, and application must be allocated based on need. The pirate's operational area has expanded to about 2.5 million square miles, but the naval area of concern is far larger. Some observers have suggested the use of satellites or high-altitude, long-endurance remotely piloted vehicles to find and track their vessels on the high seas. This would appear to be a misuse of valuable assets. There are far more important missions that will be assigned to them.

While piracy is a problem, it must be compared to other maritime issues. There are experts concerned about how piracy is being twisted and manipulated into a major problem. In one issue of the U.S. Naval Institute journal *Proceedings*, an officer stated, "While maritime piracy incidents capture media attention and generate international calls for action, the piracy threat is in fact overstated."[182] Apparently another anonymous writer concurred and stated in a later issue of *Proceedings*, "They pose little threat. But there

Figure 4. A visit, board, search, and seizure team assigned to guided-missile destroyer USS Kidd board the Iranian-flagged fishing dhow Al Molai. The team detained 15 suspected pirates, who were holding a 13-member Iranian crew hostage for several weeks. U.S. Navy photo.

is peril in comparing them to Barbary brigands. That muddies the debate—clouding our perspective on what truly is in our national interest."[183]

It was noted earlier that that Barbary pirates were impacting American commerce. In fact, the ransoms paid at that time greatly exceeded those extorted today when the cost is amortized over time. The same author indicates that less than one percent of container traffic from Asia and headed to the East Coast passes through the Suez Canal. They cross the Pacific Ocean and use the Panama Canal to bring their goods. Most Middle East oil tankers bound for the U.S. sail past the Cape of Good Hope rather than Suez as the best business practices, not because of pirates. They also noted that the U.S. is the third largest exporter in the world behind China and Germany. The point was that the American internal market was "so large only about one percent of U.S. businesses even view the export market as a target."[184] Conversely, the Barbary pirates were hurting the American economy, and thus warranted a harsh response. The impact of today's pirates pales by comparison.

As with maritime piracy, other forms of piracy tend to flourish in under-governed areas, which may be real physical terrain; or in the case of intellectual property, in virtual domains or cyberspace. For perspective, according to the Office of Management and Budget, intellectual property piracy costs the

U.S. an estimated $58 billion per year, or near an order of magnitude higher than all the costs associated with maritime piracy.[185] Described earlier were the fatal consequences of fake prescription drugs, not to mention the loss of revenue to the pharmaceutical companies. There are many other examples of piracies that could be cited. The intent of listing these few examples is to acknowledge that countering all forms of piracy is a zero-sum game finitely bounded by resource constraints. These examples confirm that asking questions of the strategic importance of maritime piracy is quite legitimate. Were it not for more important naval missions in the HOA waters, continued involvement at current levels could be hard to justify. That is especially true when considering the following section and the total costs that could be incurred.

Going Ashore

As the Marines' Hymn recounts, the Barbary pirates were defeated by invasion of "the shores of Tripoli." In fact, piracy only flourishes when it either supported by local governments or operates in areas that are ungoverned or under-governed. Most analysts of counter-piracy agree that eliminating the support mechanisms is the best way to tackle the problem. Fighting pirates on the high seas is dealing with the symptoms, and ones that can be constantly regenerated. As previously indicated, there are issues of boundaries, and many countries involved with the counter-piracy coalition are very concerned about armed forces escalating their commitment for land operations. Some politicians view this as the abhorred *mission creep.*[186]

While direct action against pirates on land is one course of action, there are many more options that can be considered, and they may have significant implications for SOF. Included would be a host of civil-military missions among which would be support of training to enhance the capacity of local and regional law enforcement and military forces. Other operations would include providing medical support and small construction projects such as schools and bridges. Of course, digging wells for water which is critical in those countries would be included. To be effective, the scope of these activities would expand well beyond what is currently provided. This is not new and the outstanding efforts put forth in Operation Enduring Freedom - Horn of Africa (OEF-HOA) (Djibouti) deserve recognition.[187] However, far more resources would be required to accomplish the objectives of reducing or eliminating piracy. It is also noted that there is a need for security interventions to be tied to development aid for the process to be seen as legitimate by nation involved.[188] As Assistant Secretary of State for Political Military Affairs, Andrew Shapiro correctly stated:

> Realistically, there will be no end to piracy at sea until there is some degree of political stability and economic recovery ashore in Somalia, including local governmental authorities with the ability to enforce law and order both on land and at sea. We believe supporting the re-establishment of stability and adequate governance in Somalia represents the only sustainable long-term solution to piracy.[189]

In 2010, the DOS articulated a "dual track" approach to Somalia.[190] That meant that instead of only supporting the relatively dysfunctional Transitional Federal Government, which has been plagued by constant turnover of key personnel, they would also include assistance to the local governments of Puntland, Somaliland, and the clans of southern Somalia. Certainly, improved governance in Puntland would be important as many of the pirates operate from bases in that region. The EU has also noted their geopolitical strategic interests in the HOA and their historic engagement with the countries of the region. The EU indicated a desire to support the welfare of the people and help lift them from poverty into self-sustaining economic growth, and the need to protect its own citizens from the threats that emanate from some parts of the region. Their goal is stated, "To achieve its objective of peace, stability, security, prosperity and accountable government."[191] It is important to note they are not just addressing Somalia, but instead a rather large region including three landlocked nations. When the EU talks of the HOA, it is defined as "the countries belonging to the Inter-Governmental Authority for Development (IGAD) – Djibouti, Eritrea, Ethiopia, Kenya, Somalia, Sudan, South Sudan and Uganda."[192]

Ambitious in scope, Western nations recognize the seriousness of the piracy problem but seem to have articulated unrealistic commitments. Specifically, none of them address the economic realities of their current fiscal situations. The EU is in crisis with one economic calamity after another and with no projection of stability for years to come. Similarly the U.S. still has severe economic problems and is vulnerable to the economic fluctuations of Europe.[193] Further, there is great political pressure to fix our internal infrastructure problems before sending more money abroad. The point is that nation building is expensive, but nation building is exactly what is being described in all of those policy statements. The question of will and resources was one of the key findings from a 2009 workshop at the Naval War College. Specifically they stated, "Proposals to stop piracy by 'fixing' Somalia, however, beg the question—it is doubtful the international community has the capability or will to transform Somalia quickly into a stable and viable state."[194] Unfortunately the conditions for providing the resources that would be necessary to enhance stability in the HOA have deteriorated, but the recommendations keep coming.

Several articles in the *U.S. Naval Institute Proceedings* have carried the theme of conducting counter-piracy operations by altering the dynamics in the surrounding region. In 2010, David Axe noted the connection between Somali pirates and Kenya in that some of the successful pirates moved their homes to Kenya to protect their ill-gotten gains. Axe called for actions "hitting them where they live."[195] Commander Joshua Himes addressed "A New Approach to Piracy," indicating "We need to change the conventional wisdom on ship hijacking and take the fight ashore."[196] His concept supports a law enforcement effort and "and an aggressive legal agenda." Rather than focusing on the pirates, or foot soldiers, as they are called, the emphasis should be on attacking the supporting structure of financiers, or negotiators. Himes stresses the need for financial network forensic development, but does acknowledge the difficulties of penetrating a cash-based system heavily reliant on personal relationships (Hawala).[197]

Should direct action options be more vigorously employed, a number of complicated questions with long-term consequences will have to be addressed. From history we know it is likely that the rules almost assuredly will remain in a state of flux, thus placing considerable burden on commanders charged with operational responsibilities. Considerations would include; can troops be inserted; if so, how many and for how long? When do hostage-rescue missions (as now authorized under some conditions) become raids (with emphasis on killing pirates or destroying their facilities)? How long does a raid/rescue last before it is an invasion? Is an effort made to capture pirates; and if so what is done with them? Are they to be turned over to local authorities, taken to international courts, or returned to the U.S. for trial? What are the limitations, if any, on weapons that can be used? What responsibilities are assumed for collateral casualties, and what legal courses are afforded them for redress? While the laws of counter-piracy are a century and a half old, it is essential that the laws and potential administrative constraints be determined before more actions are taken. That is not a burden that should be levied on an ever-changing international command structure.

9. The Next Move

One can only speculate as to what will come next, but if past is pro-logue, then certain evolutionary trends are somewhat predictable. Over the past decade, pirates and counter-piracy elements in the HOA have been partaking in a complex and dangerous dance. While beginning as simple robbery at sea by inexperienced thugs taking advantage of operating from ungoverned territory, the huge and ever-escalating profit motive has attracted other players. Investors emerged to provide the willing young pirates with better weaponry and ships capable of venturing much farther from their Puntland bases at the tip of the horn in Somalia. The DOS formally noted, "Piracy has gone from a fairly ad hoc disorganized criminal endeavor to a highly developed transnational criminal enterprise."[198] As indicated earlier, those advanced capabilities allowed these seagoing criminals to nearly double their operational area, which complicates the searches by counter-piracy forces.

The logical nexus between terrorist organizations, organized crime, and local pirates has begun to unfold. Somalia remains in turmoil with a weak central government in Mogadishu that is frequently under attack, and a civil war has engulfed most of the southern part of the country. The transitional government would probably falter and fail without considerable support from the African Union. Exacerbating the situation has been extensive famine that frequently plagues that region. Extreme poverty fuels the Islamist factions vying for power, and the terrorist organization of al-Shabaab waxes and wanes as they expand their attacks into Kenya and Uganda.[199] While external assistance is necessary to maintain any level of governmental stability, it also poses a conundrum. The mere vocal support for the Transitional Federal Government by the United States and others has caused considerable resentment among many segments of the local population and led to increased recruiting for al-Shabaab.

While initially very weak and predominantly ideological, al-Shabaab does have ties to al-Qaeda that have increased over time. Those tentacles are very long and reach back into the United States via Somali ex-patriots living there. There have been several reports of Americans, such as Dahir Gurey Sheikh Ali Guled, being killed in various engagements in Somalia.[200] Al-Shabaab has sheltered known al-Qaeda operatives and provided training bases for them. International in nature, many of their personnel come with considerable combat experience from Iraq, Pakistan, and Afghanistan.[201] Of particular concern is their demonstrated ability to follow through on threats and an intense hatred of the United States.

As a counter move, the U.S. has started offering very large rewards for the capture of specifically identified leaders of al-Shabaab also known as Harakat Shabaab al-Mujahidin. In a formal announcement, the DOS noted, "The al-Shabaab organization's terrorist activities pose a threat to the stability of East Africa and to the national security interests of the United States."[202]

Figure 5. A visit, board, search, and seizure team from guided-missile cruiser USS Anzio investigates a suspected pirate skiff. U.S. Navy photo by Mass Communication Specialist 2nd Class Bryan Weyers.

While piracy in the HOA vicinity generally comes from Somalia, there is a potential connection to al-Qaeda in the Arabian Peninsula (AQAP) that is worth considering. Headquartered in Yemen, AQAP is thought by some counterterrorism analysts as the most active and lethal al-Qaeda affiliate, and they are intent on striking at both the U.S. homeland and regional targets.[203] In May 2012, they demonstrated their ability to strike in Yemen's capital, Sanaa. In a suicide attack, a massive explosion was carried out by a man in a military uniform in the middle of the tightly-packed parade rehearsal. The bomb killed more than 90 people and wounded at least 220 others.[204]

In fact, AQAP has been considered the most pressing terrorist threat to America, and a very aggressive campaign has been launched to counter that organization. In particular there have been very effective strikes conducted by armed remotely piloted vehicles, often launched from nearby HOA countries.[205] As in Somalia where al-Shabaab, which can be considered an insurgency with a goal of overthrowing the existing government, is tied to al-Qaeda, the same is true in Yemen. AQAP is closely affiliated with insurgents attempting to overthrow that government. The obvious problem in both areas is how to engage in counterterrorism without becoming entangled in local counterinsurgency operations. The authorized remotely piloted vehicle attacks, designed for targeted killings, eliminate elements of both organizations as they are nearly indistinguishable. However, they sometimes cause collateral casualties. Such events have unintended consequences including resentment that leads to increased recruitment.

Many strategic analysts view al-Qaeda as having a franchised organizational structure. Referred to as AQAM, the sub-elements follow a general ideology but may vary in objectives and execution. According to Richard Shultz, "al-Qaeda believes it is engaged in a global millenarian clash with the United States and more broadly the West."[206] That suggests that while various elements of al-Qaeda conduct local terrorist attacks, there is a common strategic goal to attack with a worldwide jihad in all possible venues, including Western economic systems. The 2012 RAND study on maritime irregular warfare specifically warned about the nexus of jihadists and pirates. Regarding camps in Pakistan, Yemen, and Somalia, they stated "agencies should also work to prevent jihadists from joining forces in the HOA region."[207] It appears that liaison has begun. Though some observers claim that al-Qaeda has problems making inroads with the Somali clans, they have been somewhat successful with their counterparts in al-Shabaab. Colonel John Steed, the principal military adviser to the UN special envoy to Somalia and head of the envoy's counter-piracy unit, states "There is a growing link and growing cooperation between al-Shabaab who are desperate for funding and resources with other criminal gangs and with pirates."[208]

It does not require extensive physical damage to have major impact on those economic systems. The effects of the 9/11 attacks are still reverberating and at a total cost in trillions of dollars.[209] Exploiting Western financial vulnerabilities was one of the objectives of those attacks, and they succeeded beyond their wildest dreams. When comparing the total expense of planning and executing those attacks against the enormous fiscal damage incurred, the cost effectiveness ratio for al-Qaeda is estimated at over seven million to one. Terrorist organizations in the area have used such methods before. On 17 November 1997, the Islamic Group and Jihad Talaat al-Fath attacked tourists near the Egyptian archeological site near Luxor. The gunmen executed 62 people and dealt a crippling blow to the Egyptian economy and cutting the critical tourism industry by at least 50 percent.[210] While reports vary regarding inter-organizational relationships, the DOS believes there is a connection between the Egyptian Islamist groups and al-Qaeda.

These examples demonstrate that al-Qaeda has already employed attacks against economic targets as an effective tool. The concern, therefore, is that they will take advantage of the increasing capabilities of pirates in the HOA and make a more concerted effort to interrupt the flow of goods through those strategic waterways. The terrorists already benefit from the revenue produced by pirates. That they would invest in upgrading the weapons available is a logical countermeasure to armed ship riders carrying only small arms. For example, they could provide anti-ship rockets or convert existing shoulder-launched anti-armor weapons to be used against ships. These include weapons with far greater destructive power that the RPGs pirates currently carry. Imagine a Javelin-equivalent weapon in the hands of pirates and the effect that could have on cargo ship defenses.[211]

Other analysts have suggested that non-state actors may take control of terrain near the naval choke points and critical coastal waters. From there they would have the capability to launch much heavier anti-ship missiles.[212] George Friedman argues this is the next logical step in piracy. If territorial control is afforded to aggressive non-state actors, even on a temporary basis, their ability to disrupt shipping would increase dramatically. Transient alliances between ideologically-based organizations and financially-motivated pirates would likely occur. The former, such as AQAM, may gain access to more advanced technology, including unmanned underwater vehicles that are currently being developed by several countries.[213] These unmanned underwater vehicles could pose a significant threat to commercial vessels. Employment requires a degree of sophistication that has not yet been observed in AQAM elements. Yet, they cannot be discounted as AQAM elements have proven to be quite innovative and adaptive. Should any of these eventualities occur, then the situation has moved from piracy to maritime irregular warfare, now referred to as confronting irregular challenges.[214] If so, the role of SOF could increase dramatically.

Implications for SOF

Examples of SOF interventions in counter-piracy have been cited. There is no doubt that SOF elements have the capabilities required for many counter-piracy missions, especially for maritime hostage-rescue operations. They have been adequately demonstrated on multiple occasions. The more fundamental question is to what extent these valuable resources should be dedicated to counter-piracy missions? Participation will be governed by resource allocation, risk management, and political exigencies. Political considerations may not be desirable to operators, or the best use of SOF, however, public interest and perceived concerns will influence decisions to employ military forces.

Some experienced officials in the SOF community make a definite and important distinction between counter-piracy and hostage-rescue operations. From interviews with SEALs who recently had operated in the HOA region, it was clear that government counter-piracy per se was viewed as a mission for conventional naval forces. Patrolling the seas and apprehending pirates operating there will continue as an international cooperative effort by traditional surface naval forces.[215] However, SOF support will be required for various specific missions, and not all will be conducted by SEALs.

Much of countering piracy depends on the capabilities of government agencies based in the contiguous area. Important are the military and law enforcement elements and their ability to exert control over their territory both on land and water. Therefore, foreign internal development missions by other SOF elements would be appropriate. Supported by civil affairs elements, basic training of the host military and police will be important. Note that while personnel come from United States Army Civil Affairs and Psychological Operations Command (Airborne), there are currently 20 projects underway in five HOA countries, Kenya, Ethiopia, Comoros, Uganda, and Djibouti.[216] Most experts agree that civil-military operations working in conjunction with traditional naval forces will be more important than direct action in containing pirate activities.[217]

Also noted has been a confluence of piracy with irregular warfare and terrorism. A common factor for those involved is the use of coastlines and internal waterways for transportation and staging attacks. The U.S. Navy Special Boat Units have been engaged in assisting host nations to develop increased capacity to counter these activities. That will continue and is likely to increase. As recommended by RAND's maritime irregular warfare study, care must be taken to provide capabilities at a level that can be maintained by local authorities when advisers leave.[218]

One direct action skill set that must be maintained is the ability to retake ships that have been captured and are held by pirates. The types of vessels may range from large tankers and cargo ships to private yachts. Unfortunately, the effectiveness of prior rescues has caused pirates to become more violent and willing to kill hostages quickly should negotiations deteriorate or they sense an impending attack. While simply attempting to take hostages for ransom, smaller craft, such as the Le Pocant, or fishing boats, are easier prey than large cargo ships that may be employing armed ship riders. While some of these incidents may be resolved by intervention of traditional naval forces, ones requiring surreptitious boarding may well require SOF expertise.

Hostage for ransom pirates will probably stay away from attempting to take cruise ships as the logistics of handling large numbers of people significantly complicates their efforts. However, opportunistic pirates have made a few unsuccessful attempts. Not well educated, the attackers probably did not consider the exhausting consequences had they been successful in boarding. Of greater concern should be that terrorists may be targeting cruise liners, in which case large numbers of hostages is seen by them as an advantage. Chechen rebels have already demonstrated such tactics on land with the taking of the Nord Ost Theater in Moscow in 2002, and their attack of the school in Beslan in the north Caucus region of the Russian Federation in 2004.[219] The terrorist takeover of the Achille Lauro in 1985 proved the viability of capturing a cruise ship.[220] The difference in those attacks was that the Chechen terrorists were suicidal and prepared to die with their hostages. The Jackal-inspired Palestine Liberation Organization terrorist attack led by Abu Abbas intended to negotiate and live. The combination of suicidal terrorists holding a cruise ship would be one of the most challenging hostage rescue operations that could be contemplated.

While direct action missions, especially hostage-rescue, will continue, the options for taking the conflict ashore suggests that indirect actions will increase significantly. These are natural extensions of SOF capabilities. High priority would be given to both civil affairs and foreign internal defense, including the training of military and police organizations. These actions would be aimed at increasing local capacity for establishing and maintaining regional stability. As the Somali governmental infrastructure is woefully inadequate, it is certain that all military involvement would be coordinated with efforts by the DOS and international agencies working jointly to improve conditions in the HOA. An important question for USSOCOM, as well as USAFRICOM and USCENTCOM is the amount of SOF resources that can be committed to counter-piracy at any given time. While most analysts and political leaders would agree that such efforts would be cost-effective in the long run, commitments must be compared against global realities. There is a high probability that much of the training requirements would be contracted to civilian firms. As has been experienced before, that can be a double edged sword as companies and the military compete for the same personnel resources.

The issues of boundaries were discussed earlier and also have SOF implications. By the very nature of most SOF operations, complex coordination is inherent.

Summary

As old as seafaring, piracy remains a global problem, one that never will be totally eliminated. For the past decade, the escalating attacks in the HOA have been the focus of attention for both international governmental organizations and the reporting of the media. Once conducted by ragtag bunches of young thugs, their windfall profits soared from about $150,000 per ship to $5 million and more. Spurred by success, they have spawned advanced institutional structures and can be considered akin to entrepreneurial enterprises of organized crime. A few years ago, few strategists would have foreseen emergence of a stock market and investors, or a network composed of translators and negotiators devoted solely to supporting piracy. Their intra-clan relationships, and use of alternative financial mechanisms, like Hawala, have made their structures extremely difficult to penetrate or eliminate. Because of the support of those investors, pirates have been able to purchase, or steal, larger vessels that are used as mother-ships. Use of those larger crafts have allowed them to sail greater distances, and in a short time they have been able to double their operational area to well over 2.5 million square miles.

At present, their primary objective is to take ships and hold them and the crew for ransom rather than seizing cargo for resale. Piracy in other areas, such as off West Africa, often targets the cargo which is stolen and sold on the black market. That theft objective is more dangerous for crew members as they do not hold value as live hostages. For a variety of reasons, in recent years pirates have become more violent on both coasts of the continent.

There is no doubt that piracy has had a financial impact on the shipping industry. It is estimated that it cost them over $7 billion in 2011. It is noteworthy that while well over $100 million was paid in ransom that year, the majority of the extra costs were in piracy avoidance techniques such as increased speed with attendant fuel prices, longer routes, and security guards. Still there is considerable debate regarding whether or not this is strategic issue and worth the resources. According to the International Maritime Organization, maritime shipping accounts for 90 percent of the world's international trade, and there are over 50,000 registered merchant cargo vessels. Pirates attack a few hundred of these ships per year and are rarely successful in capturing their prey. The exact number of attacks is hard to know as some incidents go unreported. When amortized against the vast extent of the shipping industry, the probability of being taken by pirates is extremely small. Countering that argument are the emotional tales of the victims and an innate sense of moral outrage at this blatant criminal activity. No doubt the media plays a significant role in keeping accounts of pirate attacks in the minds of both the public and policymakers.

Many nations have joined together to combat piracy, especially in the waters surrounding the HOA, but stretching nearly to India. The Combined Task Force 151 and other international naval forces patrol the area constantly and have been successful in arresting many pirates. What to do with them is another matter, as a large majority of those prisoners are eventually released without charges. From a U.S. strategic perspective, maintaining a fleet in the area is essential for ensuring the safety of ships transiting the Straits of Hormuz. Counter-piracy is an important, but secondary concern.

The shipping industry has also increased their protective measures. In addition to the avoidance techniques mentioned above, many have chosen to employ armed guards or ship riders. Viewed as controversial by some analysts, they have been effective in preventing pirates from boarding any of the ships they have guarded. Concerns of excessive or indiscriminate use of force have plagued private security firms since Iraq and former SEALs point to the necessity for experience in maritime warfare. Another view is that use of armed intervention by a small number of guards will lead to increased violence by the pirates. Properly trained, ship riders are an effective means of preventing a ship from falling into the hands of the seaborne criminals.

The payment of ransom is an extremely controversial matter. Deemed illegal by some countries, considered unwise and encouraging by many theoreticians, it remains at the heart of the problem. Despite policy and law, even if it precipitates additional incidents, ransom is often paid as the plight of the immediate victims outweighs the opposing philosophical rationale. Because of the controversy, the amount of ransom that has been delivered to pirates is unclear. In general, those paying admit neither to the exchange nor a monetary figure. What is known is that some form of transaction takes place, and then the ship with crew usually are released in relatively good physical condition.

There is an increasing nexus between pirate organizations, al-Shabaab, and AQAM. It is known that funding from ransom is used to assist in financing terrorist organizations. That is part of the rationale for prohibiting ransom payments when Americans are involved in any step along the way. There are logical links between piracy and other illicit operations of organized crime such as weapons trade and drug smuggling. Though personal clan relationships complicate the problem, when large amounts of money need to be laundered, then it exposes vulnerabilities that can be exploited by international financial crimes units. In this monograph, extrapolation of a trend toward a more dangerous confluence between piracy and AQAM was postulated. If proven accurate, that mandates a more strategic approach for counter-piracy operations. The time for consideration of those eventualities is now. Clearly, SOF would play an important role in the planning and execution of those missions and represent a significant shift in thinking.

Currently, SOF personnel generally view counter-piracy operations as traditional Navy or law enforcement missions. The SEALs interviewed made a clear distinction between counter-piracy and hostage-rescue operations. Their high-profile, direct-action missions, such as the rescue of Captain Phillips of the Maersk Alabama, and freeing of two kidnapped civilians held in Somalia in 2012 have demonstrated conclusively their capabilities to execute such difficult missions. But there are other issues to be addressed if strategic intervention is required. Most analysts and policymakers concur that piracy cannot be stopped by arresting culprits at sea. Rather, the fight must be taken on land. Building capacity of local and national governments is a critical component of such engagements. Execution requires application of indirect methods, ones that many SOF elements are uniquely qualified to perform. Training of indigenous military and law enforcement elements fits well within the foreign internal defense missions. Similarly, extensive civil-military operations to gain trust and confidence while bolstering support for duly constituted authority will play a significant role. The political will and providing the resources to intercede are questions for national leaders, but preparing for contingencies is a USSOCOM responsibility. The choice of mission acceptance probably will not be determined by SOF commanders, but rather directed by political leaders. Counter-piracy, therefore, should be included in a broad sense of the concept in SOF planning for future engagements. ⬆

Endnotes

1. "The Economic Cost of Somali Piracy 2011" *Oceans Beyond Piracy*, http://oceans-beyondpiracy.org/sites/default/files/economic_cost_of_piracy_2011_summary.pdf.
2. Bernd Debusmann, "The business case for high-seas piracy," *Reuters*, 26 November 2008, http://blogs.reuters.com/great-debate/2008/11/26/the-business-case-for-high-seas-piracy/.
3. Cdr. Joshua Himes, "A New Approach to Piracy," *U.S. Naval Institute Proceedings Magazine*, October 2011 Vol.137/10/1.304, http://www.usni.org/magazines/proceedings/2011-10/new-approach-piracy.
4. "Somali pirates net $170m in ransoms," News24, 23 February 2012, http://www.news24.com/Africa/news/Somali-pirates-net-170m-in-ransom-20120222.
5. "Sea piracy falls to 5-year low in 2012," *News* 24, 16 January 2013, http://www.news24.com/Africa/News/Sea-piracy-falls-to-5-year-low-in-2012-20130116.
6. Miha Hribernik, "Countering Maritime Piracy and Robbery in Southeast Asia," Briefing Paper 13/2, European Institute for Asian Studies, March 2013, http://www.eias.org/publication/briefing-paper/countering-maritime-piracy-and-robbery-southeast-asia-role-recaap?goback=%2Egde_1783225_member_219309175.
7. Robbie Corey-Boulet, "Report: Piracy in West Africa outstrips Somalia," Associated Press, 18 June 2013, http://www.utsandiego.com/news/2013/jun/18/report-piracy-in-west-africa-outstrips-somalia/.
8. Richard H. Shultz, "Strategic Culture and Strategic Studies: An Alternative Framework for Assessing al-Qaeda and the Global Jihad Movement," *JSOU Report* 12-4, May 2012.
9. Part VII, Article 101, United Nations Convention on Law of the Seas, Adopted 10 December 1982.
10. Anonymous, "Two Faces of High Seas Crime," *U.S. Naval Institute Proceedings Magazine*, July 2010 Vol. 136/7/1.289 http://www.usni.org/magazines/proceedings/2010-07/two-faces-high-seas-crime.
11. UN Convention on LOS under Part VII Article 106.
12. Paul Toscano, "The dangerous world of counterfeit prescription drugs," *USAToday*, 7 October 2011, http://www.usatoday.com/money/industries/health/drugs/story/2011-10-09/cnbc-drugs/50690880/1.
13. John C. Payne, Piracy Today: Fighting Villainy on the High Seas, Sheridan House, 2010.
14. "Piracy Timeline," Pirates Hold- Pirate History and Beyond, http://pirateshold.buccaneersoft.com/pirate_timeline.html, accessed 17 February 2012.

15. Angus Konstam, Piracy: A Complete History, Osprey Publishing, Oxford, United Kingdom, 2008.

16. Leoneda Inge, "Historians Link Pirate Ships and Slave Vessels," National Public Radio, 15 March 2007, http://www.npr.org/templates/story/story.php?storyId=8925862.

17. "Barbary Pirates," Encyclopedia Britannica, 1911, http://penelope.uchicago.edu/Thayer/E/Gazetteer/Topics/history/American_and_Military/Barbary_Pirates/Britannica_1911*.html, accessed 21 February 2012.

18. Davis, Robert C., Christian Slaves, Muslim Masters: White Slavery in the Mediterranean, The Barbary Coast, and Italy, 1500-1800. Palgrave Macmillan, New York. 2003.

19. Gerald W. Gawalt, "America and the Barbary Pirates: An International Battle against an Unconventional Foe," The Jefferson Papers, Library of Congress, http://memory.loc.gov/ammem/collections/jefferson_papers/mtjprece.html.

20. Anonymous, "The Big Myth of Somali Pirates," U.S. Naval Institute Proceedings Magazine, December 2010 Vol.136/12/1.294, http://www.usni.org/magazines/proceedings/2010-12/big-myth-somali-pirates.

21. Gawalt, Op Cit.

22. Yingying Deng, "China's Legal Enforcement on Anti-Piracy in South China Sea, " National Institute for South China Sea Studies, 2010, ccsenet.org/journal/index.php/ass/article/download/6229/4925.

23. Trinh Hoi, "Horrible Statistics of the Thai Pirates vs Vietnamese Refugees," Archives of Vietnamese Boat People, http://www.vietka.com/Vietnamese_Boat_People/HorribleStatistics.htm, accessed 20 February 2012.

24. Seth Faison, "Pirates, With Speedboats, Reign in China Sea Port," The New York Times, 20 April 1997, http://www.nytimes.com/1997/04/20/world/pirates-with-speedboats-reign-in-china-sea-port.html?pagewanted=all&src=pm.

25. Anthony Davis, "Piracy in Southeast Asia shows signs of increased organization", Jane's Intelligence Review, 1 June 2004, p. 2.

26. Catherine Zara Raymond, "Piracy and Armed Robbery in the Malacca Strait: A Problem Solved?" Naval War College Review, Summer 2008, Vol. 62 No.3, http://www.usnwc.edu/getattachment/7835607e-388c-4e70-baf1-b00e9fb443f1/Piracy-and-Armed-Robbery-in-the-Malacca-Strait--A-.

27. Jeffrey Gentleman, "Somalia Pirates Capture Tanks and Global Notice," The New York Times, 26 September 2008, http://www.nytimes.com/2008/09/27/world/africa/27pirates.html?pagewanted=all.

28. "Somali pirates 'free arms ship'" BBC News, 5 February 2009, http://news.bbc.co.uk/2/hi/africa/7871510.stm.

29. Barbara Surk, "Somali pirates seize supertanker loaded with crude," Associated Press, 17 November 2008, http://www.webcitation.org/5cTY6IAYX.

30. "Somali pirates drown with share of ransom from Sirius Star hijack," *The Guardian*, 10 January 2009, http://www.guardian.co.uk/world/2009/jan/10/sirius-star-somalia-pirates-drown.

31. William Langewiesche, "The Pirate Latitudes," *Vanity Fair*, April 2009, http://www.vanityfair.com/politics/features/2009/04/somali-pirates200904.

32. "France: Pirates Captured, Hostages Freed," *Associated Press*, 11 February 2009, http://www.cbsnews.com/2100-202_162-4009248.html.

33. Tom Phillips, "Brazil creating anti-pirate force after spate of attacks on Amazon riverboats," *The Guardian*, 17 June 2011, http://www.guardian.co.uk/world/2011/jun/17/brazil-amazon-pirates.

34. "'Pirates' raid Japanese trawler off Peru coast," *Associate Press*, 6 March 2011, http://www.google.com/hostednews/afp/article/ALeqM5h-2QuCOq8ZyexfQTSPZ_3ZBfzTbw?docId=CNG.7131e2b502649c227658543dce51e738.81.

35. Associated Press, "Nigeria: Piracy Rises Off West Africa" *The New York Times*, 11 August 2011, http://www.nytimes.com/2011/08/12/world/africa/12briefs-Nigeria.html.

36. "2011 Piracy Attacks Totaled 439; 275 off Somalia: ICC/IMB Report," Insurance Journal, 19 January 2012, http://www.insurancejournal.com/news/international/2012/01/19/231822.htm.

37. John B. Alexander, "Africa: Irregular Warfare on the Dark Continent," *JSOU Report* 09-5, May 2009.

38. "Nigeria's Boko Haram Islamic militant group on the rise," *United Press International*, 21 February 2012, http://www.upi.com/Top_News/Special/2012/02/21/Nigerias-Boko-Haram-Islamic-militant-group-on-the-rise/UPI-83451329856122/.

39. For extensive coverage on this topic see "Confronting the Terrorism of Boko Haram in Nigeria," by James Forest, *JSOU Report* 12-5, May 2012.

40. Associated Press, "Violence against shippers new norm off West Africa," *USAToday*, 13 February 2012, http://www.usatoday.com/news/world/story/2012-02-13/nigeria-pirate-attack/53070492/1.

41. Matt Woolsey, "Top Earning Pirates," *Forbes*, 18 September 2008, http://www.forbes.com/2008/09/18/top-earning-pirates-biz-logistics-cx_mw_0919piracy.html.

42. The majority of U.S. military publications concerning maritime piracy are found in U.S. Navy journals and many contain small sections on history. For those readers interested in learning far more about the history of piracy, highly recommended for future research is: Bruce A. Elleman, et al. "Piracy and Maritime Crime Historical and Modern Case Studies," *Center for Naval Warfare Studies Newport Paper Thirty-five*, January 2010.

43. Robert D. McFadden and Scott Shane, "In Rescue of Captain, Navy Kills 3 Pirates," *The New York Times*, 13 April 2009, www.nytimes.com/2009/04/13/world/africa/13pirates.html.

44. "Suspect in ship hijacking charged with piracy," *CNN*, 20 May 2009, http://edition.cnn.com/2009/CRIME/05/20/ny.pirate.indictment/index.html, accessed 16 September 2013.

45. "Somali Pirate Sentenced to 33 years in US Prison," *BBC News*, 16 February 2011 http://www.bbc.co.uk/news/world-us-canada-12486129.

46. Julian Barnes, "Navy SEALs rescue Hostages in Somalia," *The Wall Street Journal*, 26 January 2012, http://online.wsj.com/article/SB10001424052970203806504577 182422284560592.html.

47. Ibid.

48. "Navy SEALs Rescue Kidnapping Victims In Somalia," NPR's *All Things Considered*, 25 January 2012, http://www.npr.org/2012/01/25/145859961/navy-seals-rescue-kidnapping-victims, accessed 25 September 2013.

49. Sean Naylor, "Adm Olsen adds "lost" 5th SOF Truth to doctrine" *The Army Times*, 16 September 2009, http://www.sofcoast.com/weblog/2009/09/adm-olsen-adds-lost-5th-sof-truth-to-doctrine.html.

50. President Barrack Obama, "Notification of Special Forces Operation," sent to 112th Congress, 2d Session, House Document 112-83, 26 January 2012.

51. Jeffrey Gettleman, Eric Schmitt, and Tom Shanker, "Navy SEAL team rescues hostages from Somali pirates," *TwinCities.com*, 25 January 2012, http://www.twincities.com/minneapolis/ci_19822492.

52. Jill Reilly, "Somalia pirates threaten to kill hostage in wake of Navy SEAL rescue," *Mail Online*, 27 January 2012 http://www.dailymail.co.uk/news/article-2092575/Somalia-pirates-threaten-kill-hostage-wake-Jessica-Buchanan-Navy-SEAL-rescue.html.

53. AP Staff, "Four American Hostages Killed by Somali Pirates" *Associated Press*, 22 Feb 2011, http://www.aolnews.com/2011/02/22/four-american-hostages-killed-by-somali-pirates/.

54. RADM William Baumgartner, U.S. Coast Guard, Statement on International Efforts to Combat Maritime Piracy," Subcommittee on International Organizations, Human Rights, and Oversight, Committee on Foreign Affairs, U.S. House of Representatives, 30 April 2009.

55. "2011 Piracy Attacks Totaled 439; 275 off Somalia: ICC/IMB Report," *Insurance Journal*, 19 January 2012, http://www.insurancejournal.com/news/international/2012/01/19/231822.htm.

56. Senator Mark Kirk, "Ending Somali Piracy Against American and Allied Shipping," *Kirk Report*, 10 May 2011, http://www.kirk.senate.gov/pdfs/KirkReport-final2.pdf.

57. A Somali pirate leader in global shipping industry.

58. "Putland (sic) Police disrupt Ievoli hijackers," *Ocean Protection Services*, 3 January 2012, http://www.oceanprotectionservices.com/articles/?p=1248.

59. "Italian tanker Enrico Ievoli released from pirates," *Maritime Connector*, 24 April 2012, http://maritime-connector.com/news/security-and-piracy/italian-tanker-enrico-ievoli-released-from-pirates/.

60. Abdi Guled, "Somali Pirates Kill Hostage Over Delayed Ransom," *Associated Press*, 1 September 2012, http://www.huffingtonpost.com/2012/09/01/somali-pirates-hostage-killed_n_1848937.html.

61. "Somali Pirates Free MV Orna After 2 Years in Captivity, 6 Hostages Still Held," *The Maritime Executive*, 20 October 2012, http://www.maritime-executive.com/article/somali-pirates-free-mv-orna-after-2-years-in-captivity-6-hostages-still-held/.

62. Jo Chuter, "3 Syrian Hostages Released," *Maritime Security Review*, 14 January 2013, http://www.marsecreview.com/2013/01/3-syrian-hostages-released/.

63. Victoria Nuland, "UN Security Council Unanimously Urges Pursuit of Somali Piracy Kingpins," *U. S. Department of State*, 26 October, 2011, http://www.state.gov/r/pa/prs/ps/2011/10/176231.htm.

64. Rob Sheridan and Michelle Wiese Bockmann, "Ships Deter Pirate Stalkers By Signaling Armed Guards' Presence," *Bloomberg*, 22 May 2012 http://www.bloomberg.com/news/2012-05-22/ships-deter-pirate-stalkers-by-signaling-armed-guards-presence.html.

65. To test this information go to www.maritimetraffic.com There you will find the current data for hundreds of ships. Data on ports, including which sips are docked, can also be obtained. There are other sights that carry similar information.

66. "International Regulations for Preventing Collisions at Sea" 1972, http://en.wikisource.org/wiki/International_Regulations_for_Preventing_Collisions_at_Sea, accessed 22 May 2012.

67. "Economic Cost of Somali Piracy," *One Earth Future Foundation Working Paper*, 2012, http://oceansbeyondpiracy.org/sites/default/files/economic_cost_of_piracy_2011.pdf.

68. James Bridger, "African Piracy's Next Front," *USNI News*, 4 March 2013, http://news.usni.org/2013/03/04/african-piracys-next-front.

69. Heather Murdock, "Piracy Soars in West African Waters," Voice of America, 22 January 2013, http://www.voanews.com/content/piracy-soars-off-nigerian-coast/1588631.html.

70. Ibid.

71. "Piracy falls in 2012, but seas off East and West Africa remain dangerous, says IMB," *International Chamber of Commerce, ICC Commercial Crime Service*, 16 January 2013, http://www.icc-ccs.org/

news/836-piracy-falls-in-2012-but-seas-off-east-and-west-africa-remain-dangerous-says-imb.

72. Dianna Games, "Worsening piracy in West African seas needs urgent solutions," *Business Day Live*, 25 February 2013, http://www.bdlive.co.za/opinion/columnists/2013/02/25/worsening-piracy-in-west-african-seas-needs-urgent-solutions.

73. Gary Li, "West Africa: Increase in Gulf of Guinea Piracy Likely in Next Three Months," *Think Africa Press*, 28 January 2013, http://allafrica.com/stories/201301281648.html.

74. Michael N. Murphy, "Africa's Leaking Wound," *U.S. Naval Institute Proceedings*, March 2013, Vol. 139/3.1,321, http://www.usni.org/magazines/proceedings/2013-03/africas-leaking-wound.

75. Kristin Deasy, "Nigeria piracy: kidnappers demand $1.2 million ransom for 6 foreigners," *Global Post*, 20 February, 2013, http://www.globalpost.com/dispatch/news/regions/africa/nigeria/130220/nigeria-piracy-kidnappers-demand-12-million-ransom-6-for.

76. Hribernik op cit.

77. Arup Chanda, "Pirates in Indian Ocean bane for Indian, Bangladeshi fisherman," Xinhua, 20 October 2012, http://news.xinhuanet.com/english/world/2012-10/20/c_131918889.htm.

78. "Why Fish Piracy Persists: The Economics of Illegal, Unreported and Unregulated Fishing," Organisation for Economic Cooperation and Development 2005, http://www.imcsnet.org/imcs/docs/why_fish_piracy_persists.pdf.

79. Capt. David C. Iglesias, Office of Military Commissions-Prosecutions, Department of Defense, in conversation 25 February 2012.

80. Cdr. James Kraska, And Capt. Brian Wilson, "Piracy, Policy, And Law," *U.S. Naval Institute Proceedings*, December 2008, Vol. 134/12/1.270.

81. 18 USC Chapter 81 – Piracy and Privateering, http://www.law.cornell.edu/uscode/text/18/part-I/chapter-81.

82. Steven Jones, "Counter Piracy: Rules for the Use of Force International Legal Conference," All About Shipping, 7 March 2013, http://www.allaboutshipping.co.uk/2013/03/07/counter-piracy-rules-for-the-use-of-force-international-legal-conference-2/.

83. The slave trade, or human trafficking is an increasing problem and does involve transport by ships.

84. United Nations Convention on the Law of the Sea, Article 110, http://www.un.org/depts/los/convention_agreements/texts/unclos/unclos_e.pdf, accessed 1 March 2012.

85. Associated Press, "Military leaders, Clinton push for sea treaty," *CBS News*, 23 May 2012.

86. Kathryn Isted, "Sovereignty in the Arctic: An Analysis of Territorial Disputes & Environmental Policy Considerations," Journal of Transnational Law and Policy, Vol. 18, 2009, 343-376, http://www.law.fsu.edu/journals/transnational/vol18_2/isted.pdf.

87. "Once More on the Law of the Sea," *The New York Times*, 24 May 2012, http://www.cbsnews.com/8301-505245_162-57440135/military-leaders-clinton-push-for-sea-treaty/ http://www.nytimes.com/2012/05/25/opinion/once-more-on-the-law-of-the-sea.html.

88. Lauren Ploch, et al, "Piracy off the Horn of Africa," *Congressional Research Service* R40528, 27 April 2011, http://www.fas.org/sgp/crs/row/R40528.pdf.

89. "Russian navy 'sent Somali pirates to their death'" *The Week*, 12 May 2010, http://www.theweek.co.uk/politics/14701/russian-navy-%E2%80%98sent-somali-pirates-their-death%E2%80%99.

90. Yingying Deng, Op cit.

91. Christina Geisert, "Pirate or Criminal? A difference of location," *The Coast Guard Journal of Safety and Security at Sea*, Spring 2012, http://www.uscg.mil/proceedings/archive/2012/Vol69_No1_Spr2012.pdf.

92. Elizabeth Andersen, "Suppressing Maritime Piracy: Exploring the Options in International Law," *American Society for International Law*, October 2009, http://www.asil.org/files/suppressing-maritime-piracy.pdf.

93. Geisert op cit.

94. Mike Hixenbaugh, "Defense: Navy Actions Led to Pirate Hostage Deaths," *The Virginia Pilot*, 19 September 2012, http://www.military.com/daily-news/2012/09/19/defense-navy-actions-led-to-pirate-hostage-deaths.html.

95. "Pirate suspects sue Germany," *MarineLog*, 16 April 2009, http://www.marinelog.com/DOCS/NEWSMMIX/2009apr00164.html.

96. Matthias Gebauer, "Seeking a Fair Trial: Attorneys File Suit in Germany on Behalf of Alleged Pirates," *Der Spiegel*, 15 April 2009, http://www.spiegel.de/international/europe/seeking-a-fair-trial-attorneys-file-suit-in-germany-on-behalf-of-alleged-pirates-a-619103.html.

97. Combined Joint Task Force – Horn of Africa, Web Site, http://www.hoa.africom.mil/ accessed 20 May 2012.

98. Ibid.

99. "Update on Anti-Piracy" AFRICOM PAO, 18 February 2010, http://www.africom.mil/getArticle.asp?art=4052&lang=0.

100. "Maritime Safety and Security Seminar one piece of AFRICOM effort" *Africa Command Home Page*, 29 March 2012, http://africom.wordpress.com/2012/03/29/maritime-safety-security-africom/.

101. "MQ-9s Take Centre Stage in Victoria" *AFRICOM PAO*, 10 November 2009http://www.africom.mil/getArticle.asp?art=3706&lang=0.

102. Combined Maritime Forces, http://combinedmaritimeforces.com/about/ accessed 21 May 2012.

103. Ibid.

104. General James N. Mattis, "On the Posture of U.S. Central Command," Senate Armed Services Committee, 6 March 2012, http://www.fas.org/irp/congress/2012_hr/030612mattis.pdf.

105. Ms. Donna Hopkins, "Collaborating to Combat Piracy The Contact Group on Piracy off the Coast of Somalia," *The Coast Guard Proceedings*, Spring 2012, http://www.uscg.mil/proceedings/archive/2012/Vol69_No1_Spr2012.pdf.

106. "Wet-Foot Dry-Foot Policy" U.S. Immigration Support, http://www.usimmigrationsupport.org/wetfoot-dryfoot.html, accessed 22 May 2012.

107. "International Jurisdiction" *Bernaerts' Guide To The 1982 United Nations Convention On The Law Of The Sea*, http://www.bernaerts-sealaw.com/JURISDICTION,%20HOT%20PURSUIT.pdf, accessed 21 May 2012.

108. "Guidelines for Fresh Pursuit," Department of Energy, http://www.fas.org/nuke/guide/usa/doctrine/doe/o5632_7/o5632_7_a2_1.htm, accessed 7 June 2012.

109. Jeffery Gettleman, "Toughening Its Stand, European Union Sends Forces to Strike Somali Pirate Base," *The New York Times*, 15 May 2012, http://www.nytimes.com/2012/05/16/world/africa/european-forces-strike-pirate-base-in-somalia.html?_r=1.

110. Abdi Guled and Slobodan Lekic, "EU navy, helicopters strike pirate supply center," *Associated Press*, 15 May 2012, http://news.yahoo.com/eu-navy-helicopters-strike-pirate-supply-center-173333489.html.

111. Judy Dempsey, "The Risks of Chasing Pirates on Land," *The New York Times*, 2 April 2012, http://www.nytimes.com/2012/04/03/world/europe/03iht-letter03.html.

112. "The Economic Cost of Somali Piracy 2011," *Oceans Beyond Piracy*, The One Earth Foundation, http://oceansbeyondpiracy.org/sites/default/files/economic_cost_of_piracy_2011.pdf, accessed 23 February 2012.

113. Peter Leeson, "Piracy, Economics, and the Law," *The CIP Report*, July 2009, www.peterleeson.com/Economics_Piaracy_and_the_Law.pdf.

114. Ibid.

115. Ibid.

116. Rothrauff.

117. "Merchant ship crews held hostage in Somalia," European Union Naval Force Somalia, 20 December 2011, http://www.eunavfor.eu/2011/12/merchant-ship-crews-held-hostage-in-somalia/.

118. Abdiqani Hassan, "Somali pirates release longest-held hostages after 33 months," *Reuters*, 23 December 2012, http://www.reuters.com/article/2012/12/23/us-somalia-piracy-idUSBRE8BM08D20121223 accessed 16 September 2013.

119. Kaiji Hurlburt, "The Human Cost of Somali Piracy," *Oceans Beyond Piracy*, 6 June 2011, http://oceansbeyondpiracy.org/sites/default/files/human_cost_of_somali_piracy.pdf.

120. "This House Would Criminalize the Payment of Ransoms," *International Debate Education Association*, http://idebate.org/debatabase/debates/law-crime/house-would-criminalise-payment-ransoms, accessed 4 June 2012.

121. President Barack Obama, "Executive Order 13536 concerning Somalia: Executive Order Blocking Property of Certain Persons Contributing to the Conflict in Somalia," The White House, http://www.whitehouse.gov/the-press-office/executive-order-concerning-somalia.

122. "Hijacking the law: Somali pirate ransoms skirt American sanctions." http://www.thefreelibrary.com/Hijacking+the+law%3A+Somali+pirate+ransoms+skirt+American+sanctions.-a0263724846, accessed 4 June 2012.

123. "France: Pirates Captured, Hostages Freed," *Associated Press*, 11 February 2009, http://www.cbsnews.com/2100-202_162-4009248.html.

124. "Organised Maritime Piracy and Related Kidnapping for Ransom," *Financial Action Task Force*, July 2011, http://www.fatf-gafi.org/media/fatf/documents/reports/organised%20maritime%20piracy%20and%20related%20kidnapping%20for%20ransom.pdf.

125. Donald Sensing, "Piracy ransom cash ends up in al Qaeda hands," *Sense of Events*, 7 July 2011, http://senseofevents.blogspot.com/2011/07/piracy-ransom-cash-ends-up-in-al-qaeda.html.

126. " Piratical seizure Versus Payment of a ransom Decision of the Court of Appeal in Masefield AG v Amlin Corporate Member Ltd & Anor [2011] EWCA Civ 24" *MaritimeBlog*. Piracy, http://www.lawandsea.net/maritime/maritime_piracy_Masefield.html, accessed 30 May 2012.

127. Financial Action Task Force op cit.

128. "Hawala channels used to fund sea piracy ransom ops: FATF" *The Economic Times*, 11 April 2011.

129. Eben Kaplan, "Tracking Down Terrorist Financing," *Council on Foreign Relations*, 4 April, 2006, http://www.cfr.org/international-crime/tracking-down-terrorist-financing/p10356.

130. Andrew Mwangura & Jama Deperani, "MV Montecristo Freed by Special Operations Team," Somalia Report, 10 October 2011, http://www.somaliareport.com/index.php/post/1737/MV_Montecristo_Freed_By_Special_Operations_Team.

131. Molly Dunnigan, et al, Characterizing and Exploring the Implications of Maritime Irregular Warfare, *RAND National Defense Institute*, published by U.S. Navy, 2012.

132. John Tomoney, "Global Maritime Supply Chain Piracy: Threats and Countermeasures," *Security Management*, June 2012, http://securitymanagement.com/

article/global-maritime-supply-chain-piracy-threats-and-countermeasures-007808?page=0%2C1.

133. "Anti-Piracy Planning Chart," The United Kingdom Hydrographic Office, http://www.ukho.gov.uk/media/news/pages/antipiracychart.aspx, accessed 4 June 2012.

134. "Maersk Alabama Crewmembers Sue," *gCaptain*, 16 April 2012, http://gcaptain.com/maersk-alabama-crewmembers/?44629.

135. "CTF151: Counter-Piracy," *Combined Maritime Forces*, http://combinedmaritimeforces.com/ctf-151-counter-piracy/, accessed 20 May 2012.

136. Piracy – Menace at Sea, accessed 21 May 2012, http://www.simsl.com/Loss-Prevention-and-Safety-Training/PiracyDVD.htm.

137. Baumgartner Op Cit.

138. Gary Keen, "APS Ship Riders Program Brings Shipmates Together," *America's Navy*, 16 April 2010, http://www.navy.mil/submit/display.asp?story_id=52681.

139. "Ship Guards Trigger Clashes with Pirates," *United Press International*, 11 May 2012, http://www.upi.com/Business_News/Security-Industry/2012/05/11/Ship-guards-trigger-clashes-with-pirates/UPI-85851336752503/?spt=hs&or=si accessed 10 May 2012.

140. Lawrence P. Farrell, Jr., "Piracy: A Threat to Maritime Security and the Global Economy," *National Defense Magazine*, December 2012, http://www.nationaldefensemagazine.org/archive/2012/December/Pages/PiracyAThreattoMaritimeSecurityandtheGlobalEconomy.aspx.

141. Much of the information concerning seaborne private security was obtained through discussion with officials of American companies. Tom Rothrauff, a former U.S. Navy SEAL, and president of the Trident Group, was very helpful, as were others.

142. International Trade in Arms Regulation information is available at http://www.pmddtc.state.gov/regulations_laws/itar.html.

143. "Massive Floating Armories Filled With Weapons Are A Pirate's Sweet Dream" *The Guardian*, 10 Jan 2013, http://www.businessinsider.com/massive-floating-armories-filled-with-weapons-are-a-pirates-sweet-dream-2013-1.

144. John Reed, "Private Arsenal Ships in the Fight Against Piracy," DefenseTech, 22 March 2012, http://defensetech.org/2012/03/22/private-arsenal-ships-in-the-fight-against-piracy/.

145. The use of this technique was conveyed in private communications from a ship rider who dropped several such weapons in the waters off the coast of Kenya.

146. Rothrauff interview.

147. "India police open murder case against Italian ship crew," *BBC News*, 17 February 2012, http://www.bbc.co.uk/news/world-asia-india-17071474.

148. "Marines denied bail, Italy summons Indian envoy," *Hindustan Times*, 19 May 2012, http://www.hindustantimes.com/India-news/NewDelhi/Marines-denied-bail-Italy-summons-Indian-envoy/Article1-858403.aspx.

149. Patricia Jimenez Kwast, "Maritime Law Enforcement and the Use of Force: Reflections on the Categorisation of Forcible Action at Sea in the Light of the Guyana/Suriname Award," *Law Journal of Conflict and Security Law Volume 13*, Issue 1, Oxford Press 2008, http://jcsl.oxfordjournals.org/content/13/1/49.abstract.

150. Tullio Treves, "Piracy, Law of the Sea, and Use of Force: Developments off the Coast of Somalia," *The European Journal of International Law* Vol. 20 no. 2, 2009, http://www.ejil.org/pdfs/20/2/1800.pdf.

151. Rothrauff interview.

152. Ibid. He noted that ships often pick up cargo and drop them off as best they can. When delivering a load to a specific destination the may not be a guarantee of a return load and thus the ship may find it more economical to wait rather than sail empty.

153. Transiting the Gulf of Guinea during February 2013, the author was allowed access copies of confidential reports from *Dryad Maritime* that indicated recent activity. In fact, three pirate attacks took place while we were in the general area, but all targeted cargo ships.

154. Nic Robertson, "Documents reveal al Qaeda's plans for seizing cruise ships, carnage in Europe," *CNN* 1 May 2012, http://www.cnn.com/2012/04/30/world/al-qaeda-documents-future/index.html.

155. Ibid.

156. "Reporter executed on video," *Mail Online*, http://www.dailymail.co.uk/news/article-101564/Reporter-executed-video.html. Accessed 11 July 2013.

157. Francesco Santangelo, staff captain of the Silver Wind, in private interviews aboard the ship 16 and 20 February 2013. As second in command, Santangelo was the senior security official.

158. "Achille Lauro Hijacking Mediterranean Sea, October 1985," Special Operations.com,http://www.specialoperations.com/Images_Folder/library2/achille.htmlauro. Accessed 5 May 2012.

159. Tom Clancy and General Carl Stiner, *Shadow Warriors: Inside the Special Forces*, G.P. Putnam and Sons, 2002.

160. During the period 4 through 22 February 2013 the author was on the Silver Wind which transited waters off West Africa. All passengers received the letter mentioned. In addition private meetings were held with the second in command and counter-piracy measures discussed.

161. Once it was learned that counter-piracy training was being conducted, private interviews were held with various crew members. Rather than officers of the

ship, these were the staff members, all of whom hold extra duties for emergency situations.

162. Rothrauff interview.

163. Tomoney, Op cit.

164. "The Attack on the USS Cole" http://www.al-bab.com/yemen/cole1.htm Note an Arab web site, this reference carries a rather complete time line of the event and the following investigation.

165. The author was a member of the National Research Council Committee for Assessment of Non-Lethal Weapons Science and Technology, 2000 – 2002 The report "An Assessment of Non-Lethal Weapons Science and Technology" is available at http://www.nap.edu/catalog.php?record_id=10538.

166. The author has personal experience with these systems and has heard the clarity and directionality of the broadcast signal.

167. "I beat pirates with a hose and sonic cannon," *BBC News*, 17 May 2007 http://news.bbc.co.uk/2/hi/uk_news/6664677.stm.

168. Personal observation while transiting the Gulf of Guinea February 2013.

169. Vahan Simidian, CEO of HPV Technologies, private interview 8 March 2013. Previously the author has seen the system demonstrated at the Los Angeles County Sheriff's Office and can attest to the clarity and output of MAD systems.

170. Jeremy A. Kaplan, "Navy Shows Off Powerful New Laser Weapon," *Fox News*, 8 April 2011, http://www.foxnews.com/scitech/2011/04/08/navy-showboats-destructive-new-laser-gun/.

171. Carlo Kopp "High Energy Laser Directed Energy Weapons," Technical Report APA-TR-2008-0501, *Defense Today*, Updated April, 2012, http://www.ausair-power.net/APA-DEW-HEL-Analysis.html.

172. John B. Alexander, *Winning the War*, St. Martin's Press, 2003.

173. "Raytheon Produces Active Denial and Other Directed Energy Solutions," *Raytheon*, 3 March 2008, http://www.raytheon.com/newsroom/feature/ads_03-08/.

174. "The U.S. Navy's Vision for Confronting Irregular Challenges," *Department of the Navy*, January 2010.

175. Ibid.

176. BMP4: Best Management Practices for Protection against Somali Based Piracy (Version 4 – August 2011) Witherby Publishing Group, LTD.

177. Ibid.

178. Ibid.

179. Anthony Cordesman, "Iran, Oil, and the Strait of Hormuz," *Center for Strategic and International Studies*, 26 Mar 2007 http://csis.org/files/media/csis/pubs/070326_iranoil_hormuz.pdf.

180. Hilary Krieger "US committed to preventing Iran nuclear capability," 1 March 2012, http://www.jpost.com/DiplomacyAndPolitics/Article.aspx?id=259950.

181. Associated Press, "Iran offers mixed response to U.S. pirate rescue," *USAToday*, 7 January 2012, http://www.usatoday.com/news/world/story/2012-01-07/iran-pirate-rescue/52429426/1.

182. Anonymous, "The Overstated Threat," *U.S. Naval Institute Proceedings Magazine*, December 2008 Vol. 134/12/1.270.

183. Anonymous, "The Big Myth of Somali Pirates," *U.S. Naval Institute Proceedings Magazine*, December 2010 Vol.136/12/1.294. It is noted these articles could have been written by the same person.

184. Ibid.

185. Stephen Galloway, "Who Says Piracy Costs $58 Billion Per Year?" *The institute for Policy Innovation*, 1 May 2012, http://www.ipi.org/ipi_issues/detail/who-says-piracy-costs-58-billion-per-year.

186. Dempsey, op cit.

187. "Operation Enduring Freedom - Horn of Africa (OEF-HOA) (Djibouti)," *Global Security*, http://www.globalsecurity.org/military/ops/oef-djibouti.htm, accessed 4 June 2012.

188. Stephen Anning and M. L. R. Smith, "The Accidental Pirate: Reassessing the Legitimacy of Counterpiracy Operations" *U.S. Army War College, Parameters*, Vol XLIII, Summer 2012, http://www.carlisle.army.mil/usawc/Parameters/Articles/2012summer/Anning-Smith.pdf.

189. Andrew Shapiro, "Confronting Global Piracy," Assistant Secretary, Bureau of Political-Military Affairs Statement before the Subcommittee on Terrorism, Nonproliferation and Trade of the House Foreign Affairs Committee, Washington, DC 15 June 2011, http://london.usembassy.gov/piracy003.html.

190. Paul Mwaura, "Somalia: U.S. Top Africa Diplomat Hopeful in New 'Dual-Track' Policy," allafrica.com, 22 Oct 2010, http://allafrica.com/stories/201010230022.html.

191. "Council conclusions on the Horn of Africa," Council of the European Union, 3124th Foreign Affairs Council meeting, Brussels, Belgium, 14 November 2011, w.consilium.europa.eu/uedocs/cms_data/docs/pressdata/EN/foraff/126052.pdf.

192. Ibid.

193. Dominic Rushe & Larry Elliot, "Obama urges Europe to act swiftly to prevent economic collapse," *The Guardian*, 8 Jun 2012, http://www.guardian.co.uk/business/2012/jun/08/obama-europe-act-economic-collapse.

194. Cdr. James Kraska, "Countering Maritime Piracy: The Report on the U.S. Naval War College Workshop on Somali Piracy, Fresh Thinking for an Old Threat," International Law Department, U.S. Naval War College, 28 April 2009, http://www.usnwc.edu/getattachment/521cc632-2c29-4190-97d0-2d3a9dacd2c6/Countering-Maritime-Piracy.

195. David Axe, "Defeating Somali Pirates on Land: The Kenya Connection," *U.S. Naval Institute Proceedings*, 30 June 2010.

196. Cdr. Joshua Himes, "A New Approach to Piracy," *U.S. Naval Institute Proceedings*, 11 October 2011, Vol.137/10/1304, http://www.usni.org/magazines/proceedings/2011-10/new-approach-piracy.

197. Ibid.

198. Shapiro, op cit.

199. Stephanie Hanson, "Backgrounder: Al Shabaab," *Council on Foreign Relations*, 10 August 2011, http://www.cfr.org/somalia/al-shabaab/p18650.

200. Dana Hughes, "American Jihadi Killed In Somalia Shootout," *ABC News*, 10 September 2010, http://abcnews.go.com/Blotter/american-jihadi-killed-somalia-shootout/story?id=11604972#.T9Yn3NVDy5I.

201. Christopher Harnisch, "The Terror Threat from Somalia: The Internationalization of Al Shabaab," *American Enterprise Institute*, 12 February 2010, http://www.criticalthreats.org/sites/default/files/pdf_upload/analysis/CTP_Terror_Threat_From_Somalia_Shabaab_Internationalization.pdf.

202. "Rewards for Justice - al-Shabaab Leaders Reward Offers," Office of the Spokesperson, *U.S. State Department*, 7 June 2012, http://www.state.gov/r/pa/prs/ps/2012/06/191914.htm.

203. Jonathan Masters, "Backgrounder, Al-Qaeda in the Arabian Peninsula (AQAP)," *Council on Foreign Relations*, 24 May 2012, http://www.cfr.org/yemen/al-qaeda-arabian-peninsula-aqap/p9369.

204. Mohammed Ghobari, "Somber Yemen parade takes place after huge bomb attack," *Reuters*, 22 May 2012, http://www.reuters.com/article/2012/05/22/us-yemen-idUSBRE84L0VJ20120522.

205. Greg Miller, "CIA seeks new authority to expand Yemen drone campaign," *The Washington Post*, 18 April 2012, http://www.washingtonpost.com/world/national-security/cia-seeks-new-authority-to-expand-yemen-drone-campaign/2012/04/18/gIQAsaumRT_story.html.

206. Richard H. Shultz, "Strategic Culture and Strategic Studies: An Alternative Framework for Assessing al-Qaeda and the Global Jihad Movement," *JSOU Report* 12-4, May 2012.

207. Molly Dunigan, et al, Characterizing and Exploring the Implications of Maritime Irregular Warfare, " *RAND National Defense Research Institute*, 2012.

208. Jonathan Saul and Camila Reed, "Shabaab-Somali pirate links growing: UN adviser," *Reuters*, 20 October 2011, http://af.reuters.com/article/topNews/idAFJOE79J0G620111020.

209. Shan Carter and Amanda Cox, "One 9/11 Tally: $3.3 Trillion" *New York Times*, 8 September 2011, http://www.nytimes.com/interactive/2011/09/08/us/sept-11-reckoning/cost-graphic.html.

210. Holly Fletcher, "Backgrounder: Jamaat al-Islamiyya Also known as: Gama'a al-Islamiyya, Al-Gama'at; Egyptian al-Gama'at al-Islamiyya; Islamic Gama'at; Islamic Group, Jama'a Islamia'" *Council on Foreign Relations*, 30 May 2008, http://www.cfr.org/egypt/jamaat-al-islamiyya/p9156.

211. "Javelin Portable Anti-Tank Missile, United States of America," *army-technology.com*, http://www.army-technology.com/projects/javelin/, accessed 1 June 2012.

212. George Friedman, "The End of Counterinsurgency and Scalable Force," *STRATFOR*, 5 June 20012, http://www.stratfor.com/weekly/end-counterinsurgency-and-scalable-force.

213. Gareth Evans, "UUVs: Unmanned and in Demand," Navaltechonology.com, 15 October 2010, http://www.naval-technology.com/features/feature98410/.

214. "The U.S. Navy's Vision for Confronting Irregular Challenges," Department of the Navy, January 2010.

215. From interviews conducted at Coronado 4-5 April 2012.

216. MG Jeffrey Jacobs, Command Briefing, United States Army Civil Affairs and Psychological Operations Command (Airborne), http://www.civilaffairsassoc.org/CA%20Assn%20Brief-for%20CA%20ASSOC.pdf, accessed 10 June 2012.

217. Dunigan et al, op cit.

218. Dunigan, et al, op cit.

219. John B Alexander, "Convergence: Special Operations Forces and Civilian Law Enforcement," *JSOU Report* 10-6, July 2010 provides more coverage of those events.

220. General Stiner, op cit.

www.ingramcontent.com/pod-product-compliance
Lightning Source LLC
Chambersburg PA
CBHW080322290526
45790CB00005B/2140